If He Says He's Evil ... Believe Him!

Searching for True Love Can Cause Cancer

Enjoy!

Keely

If He Says He's Evil ... Believe Him!

Searching for True Love Can Cause Cancer

Written by:
Kelly Molchan

iUniverse, Inc.
New York   Bloomington

If He Says He's Evil ... Believe Him!
Searching for True Love Can Cause Cancer

iUniverse books may be ordered through booksellers or by contacting:

iUniverse
1663 Liberty Drive
Bloomington, IN 47403
www.iuniverse.com
1-800-Authors (1-800-288-4677)

ISBN: 978-1-4401-4023-5 (pbk)
ISBN: 978-1-4401-4025-9 (dj)
ISBN: 978-1-4401-4024-2 (ebk)

Library of Congress Control Number: 2009932975

Printed in the United States of America

iUniverse rev. date: 7/9/2009

Acknowledgement

Writing this book was both fun and therapeutic for me, and I hope it will be interesting, educational and entertaining for all readers. These stories could not have been written without the support of my family and friends, along with years of experiences shared among us.

First and foremost, thanks to my sister, Stephanie, for being with me from the get-go when I had no clue what was happening to me and for enduring every tear (and there were many). She was my strength and my communicator when I just couldn't do it.

Many thanks to my dear friends who continually encouraged me to keep writing and to my Aunt Pam for taking the time to edit my work.

A very special thanks to my health care professionals Dr. Kevin Bethke, Dr. Leo Gordon, Sarah Miyata and Kara Catsaros at Northwestern Memorial Hospital in Chicago. My good health I owe to them.

Although it is a woman's prerogative to change reality and write a book about it, the stories in this book have been pulled from my memory and journals and are as true and accurate as I can recall. If you recognize references to specific events and people and you don't like it, please don't take it personally. It's my story.

Most importantly, I want to thank the love of my life, Daniel T. Molchan, for his enduring patience, support, and kindness. He truly is the most caring, loving, giving man I've ever known. While you can imagine that he does not enjoy all the stories I share in this book, he understands and respects my goal to write it all down. We've gone down a long, challenging path and are delighted to build our life together with a foundation of love, trust and peace.

Contents

Chapter 1

"I can be changed by what happens to me.
I refuse to be reduced by it.
In the face of such uncertainty, believe in these two things –
You are stronger than you think, and you are not alone."
Written by Maya Angelou
Card from Aunt Linda & Uncle Duck

"I can feel that!" I say very loudly and quickly. My eyes are squeezed shut in anticipation of more pain, but he stops and gives me another shot of painkiller – that's three. Thank God! I don't want to feel anything – it is frightening enough just to be here. This whole experience is surreal. I can't believe I am actually in a hospital strapped to an operating table having a lump removed from my neck. This happens to other people, not to me. I feel strangely calm, as this must be God's way of showing me what other people go through. But this isn't a dream or my imagination – it's real.

I can't see anything, I can only hear, as my face is covered with some kind of paper tent. When they put together this set up, I thought - OH COME ON – is this necessary? Now I know. They pass a gazillion things across your face, and something could be dropped. I don't think the doctor or the nurses want to see your face or the tears, and I really didn't want to see their exchanges either. This is horrifying in itself – I appreciate the privacy actually. Hooray for the paper tent!

The doctor and nurses talk quietly in the surgical room, but I'm not asleep – I can hear them. The surgeon's beeper goes off on the desk across the room.

"Nurse, get that." Beep. Beep. She ignores him. What is she doing? Why isn't she responding? Beep. Beep.

"Nurse, please answer my pager," he says into my ear. (At least I'm distracted from the digging in my neck … but she should answer for crying out loud.) Beep. Beep.

"Nurse!!" I want to scream, "Answer the pager already or you're fired! Cripes … what on earth are you DOING??!" I am seriously irritated, impatient, hurt, confused, crying, don't belong here, and just want to go home, back to my simple, uncomplicated, easy life. Answer the pager! Besides, my surgeon needs to be concentrating on my lymph node biopsy at this very moment, not wondering who else needs him right now. I need him to pay attention to ME! The nurse takes five seconds to answer the page – no emergency. Excellent. Finally, back to me!

Why am I here on this operating table anyway with a surgeon digging out a lymph node from the left side of my neck? What am I supposed to be thinking about? How could I possibly have cancer? Why me? Other people get cancer, not me. I'm only 29 years old - OK 40 or 41, but who's counting. I'm clean and healthy – I exercise regularly, am not overweight, don't smoke, don't drink much, don't have allergies, and don't take medication or use drugs. I eat right (a little chocolate everyday IS good for you), take a daily multivitamin for women with iron, calcium, zinc and folic acid, and drink plenty of fluids (diet soda counts). I keep my things clean and in order – my condo, car, clothes, office. I am optimistic, almost always positive and smiling, and am usually quite content and happy. I believe in God, the author and creator of health and life, serving and supporting others, and being a generally helpful member of society. Cancer should not strike good-hearted, well-meaning adults, children or animals. Right?

So, I'm confused. What causes cancer? How did I get cancer? Do I seriously have it? Is it something I did? Something I consumed? Something nasty I sat on? Something that was passed on to me genetically? Stress? My doctor said he just doesn't know. The nurses say they don't know. Nobody knows anything, and I don't know what to think. I don't know what I'm supposed to feel. I don't know what to expect. I don't know what is going to happen. Turns out I don't know diddly either. I do know that I'm lost in a sea of unknowns and scared to death, which makes me feel sad and alone, brings tears to my eyes and the only outlet I have – I cry.

But as I lay here only able to think and cry about it, all of a sudden a storm blew up (as my sister and I are fond of saying), and I realize that I do know how I was stricken with this disease. My cancer was caused by an accumulation of all things evil that have happened in my lifetime. While trying to live a good, clean, wholesome life, evil kept sneaking in over the years and has developed into a malignant tumor. I'm sure of it. And if you look it up, the synonyms for "malignant" include evil, hateful, spiteful, wicked, nasty, cruel, mean and malevolent. Is it a coincidence that the last word starts with "male?" Hmm ... let me think about that!

Chapter 2

*"May you face every challenge with the courage
and confidence that come from knowing
you're deeply cared about."*
Card from friends Kris & Aymeric

The surgery is over. I'm not in pain, and I know I'm not dying, but I can't stop crying. I'm absolutely overwhelmed, emotionally exhausted, and I just don't know what to expect. I'm not in control. I'm not sobbing or anything, but the tears just flow and soak the paper underneath my head. I'm still strapped to the table, so I can't move … can't wipe my eyes or my nose. Hate that. Blink. Sniff. Blink. Blink. Sniff. Can they hear me? The paper tent is about to be taken down and tossed in the garbage, and I need to dry up in a hurry.

I don't want to embarrass myself by looking like a slobbering mess for no reason. Well, it's not really "no reason." I have cancer after all – that's traumatic and emotional regardless of what kind you have. But I want to be strong and brave and appear as if I'm handling this entire strange scenario like a trooper. I'm thinking this is just an exercise where I get to see what happens to other people who need surgery – I need to detach myself emotionally so it won't affect me. "Detach myself emotionally" reminds me of my ex-husband.

First Marriage

I was married once. Back then, it was all I wanted and nothing would keep me from it. I was so in love! My heart, my thoughts, my life belonged to this man. Oh, I had an army of red flags waving: DON'T DO IT! In fact, one flag went up in flames the night of our engagement, which I chose to ignore.

We had been dating off and on since I graduated from high school at age 18. When no engagement was forthcoming at birthday 21, 22, 23, or any Valentine's Day, Thanksgiving, Christmas or New Year's, around birthday 24, I guess one could say I was hopelessly pissed off. Enough was enough!

Out came the ultimatum, "By my birthday next year, you will ask me to marry you or we are done for the last time. I want to get on with my life!"

When time brought us to my 25th birthday, he made dinner reservations at one of the nicest restaurants in town. We both knew this would be the make it or break it night, even though neither of us mentioned it. I just knew he was finally ready – this night was going to be so romantic and wonderful, I could hardly stand it!

My heart began pounding with anticipation when I peeked through the curtains as he pulled into the driveway in his freshly waxed, shiny, red Monte Carlo. His car was hot, and he was so handsome! I ran out to greet him with a kiss and a hug, then hopped into the car, and we roared off to town.

Once we were seated and our meals were ordered, we tried unsuccessfully to casually chit-chat. We couldn't seem to find one thing to talk about. Looking and sounding distracted, nervous and awkward, my man summoned our waiter and ordered a bottle of champagne. I couldn't help but smile and giggle internally as I sat on my hands to prevent myself from jumping up and down in my chair. Within moments, our waiter was making a big production of presenting a fancy bottle to us, yet I did my best to appear as though drinking champagne was a regular occurrence for us and no big deal. (Inside, however, I knew this was a once in a lifetime, very special occurrence!!)

My heart was about to burst as the bubbly was being poured into sparkling crystal flutes. My man tried to distract me by pointing and asking, "Hey, what's going on over there?" Playing along, I turned my head and saw nothing but a vision of a three-tier, white wedding cake with red flowers being sliced and lovingly fed to me; however, I clearly heard a definitive clink. I knew without even looking that he had dropped the ring into my glass. Oh boy! We bought this ring three years ago, so I knew the beauty of what waited for me in the bottom of that flute, and I couldn't bear to wait another moment! I was so happy and excited!

He said, "You have to drink the entire glass of champagne to get to the bottom. No fishing for it."

"No problem."

I would do my best to be cool and not gulp, but I had waited forever for this moment. After I swallowed the last drop, he took my glass, dropped the ring into his palm, wiped it off, and reached for my hand across the table. Oh my gosh, this was it! This was really it!! He did not stand up; therefore, he could not walk over to kneel down on one knee beside me and profess his unending love, but I was willing to let that go.

Poised and ready for him to pour out his thoughts of love, admiration, and commitment, I held my breath. He looked into my eyes and declared nonchalantly, "If I have to marry someone, it might as well be you." (Evil)

I was on pause waiting for more ... blink, blink, blink. No tears, no eloquently prepared words, no fireworks. My heart had practically stopped beating in anticipation. What did he say? Was that my romantic proposal? Hm.

Apparently I responded in the affirmative, but I don't remember exactly. I was truly mystified by his words or lack thereof and was distracted by the bling. What kind of absurd proposal was that? Certainly it was more dismal than exciting. He slid the ring onto my finger and that was that. How horribly disappointing. I don't recall a smile, a hug, an I Love You, an inkling of joy or anything else he said. But I could stop asking about it – we were engaged. Hooray! I finally got what I wanted – we were engaged!

He drove me home in near silence, slowed down the car enough so that I could leap out, and screeched off – experiencing his first panic attack, I'm sure. I was willing to let that go, too, as I knew he would snap out of it once he got used to the idea, as I was a great catch – he would see. I would show him. I believed with all my heart and soul that once we were married, he would love me, respect me, adore me and realize that being married to me was the best thing that ever happened to him. I truly, honestly believed he would change how he felt about commitment because he loved me so much. The truth is – people don't change!

Was this his evil deed or mine? He should have said, "Sorry, I'm not ready, and I don't want to be married."

Or I should have said, "Thanks for giving me what I asked for, but I get the feeling this isn't really what you want. We should not get married." Neither of us were mature enough to recognize that we could be making a serious mistake.

As it turned out, we had a lovely wedding nearly a year later complete with everything I ever wanted. I was a happy, radiant bride with the biggest, fluffiest, most bubbly-ruffled (all the RAGE in 1990!) white dress available, five bridesmaids with bright, red, ruffley dresses and white hats carrying silk flower decorated fans, a three-tier white cake (yes, with red flowers) with a fountain underneath it, a swan ice sculpture, a room full of balloons, music, dancing, delicious buffet, and all of our friends and family celebrating with us.

By the end of our blessed day, the groom was drunk, I had a bleeding hole in my chest where my strapless bra had rubbed the skin off, and we had to be the last to leave the reception hall so no one could follow us to our hotel. AS IF. Had I not noticed the paranoia before? Not so much. I was exhausted and annoyed, yet elated to be a bride and now a wife. This was life!

Did we consummate the marriage that night? Ha! ... I'm not really sure, but I think so. What I do remember is that we had to get up early the next morning to meet our families for breakfast at our hotel before heading to the airport for our honeymoon. The alarm went off, we got up, scrambled to get ready and then realized the clock was wrong — we had two hours to kill before breakfast. At least we wouldn't be late!

My new husband was NOT a happy camper, and all I could do was say I was sorry and stay out of his way. Clearly, it was my fault the clock wasn't set correctly. Crabby boy sat on the couch and watched cartoons, doing his best not to stab me, choke me to death or speak to me. I didn't want him to be mad; I wasn't mad. But then I didn't have a hangover. Whatever -- what could I do about it?

This was a grand start to an equally grand honeymoon. Oh well, I was willing to overlook it because WE WERE MARRIED!!

Chapter 3

*"I must say you are one of the strongest
& most positive people I know.
Thank you for shining your light into my life!"*
Card handwritten by personal trainer & friend Jody

The doctor said he had successfully extracted my lymph node. That was good news, so I tried to smile.

"Do you want to see it?"

"Absolutely."

I did a fabulous job of holding back more tears while I responded. What does a cancerous lymph node look like? It looks like a reddish brown acorn-sized nut sitting in the bottom of a glass jar. Interesting. I wanted to touch it, to squeeze it between my fingers, and to see if it was as hard as it felt in my neck. But I didn't ask. That's gross and besides, I'm sure he wouldn't let me anyway. The lump is out, so now we could find out just what it was. I know it's bad, whatever it is. I can hardly wait to find out how this little nut is going to change my life. Doc stitched me up in three layers, each of which would dissolve in time. I felt fine, so I was ready to go.

My sister, Stephanie, took time off from work to meet me at the hospital to make sure I was OK. I could not imagine my life without her. While Stephanie is four years younger than I am, she experienced several monumental milestones in life before me. She had sex before me, she got engaged before me, she got married before me, she got divorced before me, and she had a life-altering disease before me (Crohn's). She is strong-willed, determined, and doesn't take crap from anyone. We deal with life's challenges very differently: I cry, she gets angry; I avoid confrontation, she says what's on her mind; I am generally optimistic,

11

she is generally pessimistic. And while I'm a head taller, I look up to her for advice, help, and friendship. Most importantly, I can count on her no matter what. I love her dearly and there isn't anything I wouldn't do for her, as there isn't anything she wouldn't do for me. I am so lucky!

We gobbled a quick breakfast before heading to work as if nothing significant just happened. Since it was October 6, 2005, we called Grandma Reese to wish her a happy 89th birthday. Thankfully, she didn't ask what we were doing together on a Thursday morning at 9:30 a.m. when we should have been at our respective jobs. Stephanie and I had decided not to tell the family about my situation until we knew exactly what I had and how it would be treated. Dealing with the news will be easier after we have all the facts.

I went about my business that day, as if it were any other day, because I was determined not to let this thing get in my way. I went to work. As luck would have it, I had started a new job in March of this year in real estate. I believe my boss is a gift sent to me directly from heaven. After my first appointment with the lymph node specialist on September 28, 2005, when I was told I had a lymphoma, I was walking down the doctor's office hallway in a daze, lost in thought and wondering what all this meant while trying not to cry about it anymore. I noticed my doctor standing in the doorway talking to someone. Much to my amazement, he was talking to my boss! She had in hand his credentials and lymphoma research – she had not only taken the time to look up this information, she had taken the time to be there for me. Of course, I had an immediate emotional breakdown complete with sobs and runny nose. Honestly, I should buy stock in Kleenex. I was so touched by her thoughtfulness and caring, I can't begin to express how much her being there meant to me. She stayed until my CT scan was scheduled for the next day, and we walked outside together. I left her with a final hug, tears streaming and nose running. Compassion overwhelms me – I break down every time.

My neck was bandaged and cleverly hidden underneath my turtleneck sweater, and only a select few co-workers knew about my dilemma. As the painkiller wore off, I could definitely feel the unpleasant pain in my neck increasing. The sensation was such that

I could actually feel the emptiness where the lymph node had been removed, much like feeling the space of a lost tooth with your tongue. Very strange indeed. Regardless, I had things to do. After work I helped with a mailing project for a charity and then went to a work-related event in Greek Town. I needed my life to stay as normal as possible.

Husband

The constant pain in my neck reminded me of my marriage. After our first challenging year together, we were like that hall sex joke. When we were first together, we couldn't pass each other in the hall without wanting to fuck; by the end of year one, we couldn't pass each other in the hall without wanting to say fuck you. Ha! Horrible! I don't enjoy hearing or saying the "F" word – unless I'm driving, then it can't be helped. I don't know why. But I guess it's because most people are inconsiderate, terrible drivers – and usually on their cell phones. How come I seem to be the ONLY person in Chicago ticketed for this offense? I see people in their vehicles every single day with a cell phone plastered to their ears and have never once seen a cop pull THEM over. Actually, a co-worker was pulled over for talking on her phone. She flirted and sweet-talked her way out of a ticket, which is something I would never allow myself to do. In fact, I guess I should be thankful I didn't get an additional ticket for refusing to look at or even speak to the officer who pulled me over. Ridiculous!

Anyway, we had become more like roommates than husband and wife. We rarely did things together, didn't really talk, and I wasn't allowed to ask questions because he didn't have to "report" to me. Report?! All I wanted was a little common courtesy and communication. I felt alone and miserable and had no idea what to do about it. Obviously, we had not taken the class on "What Marriage Is." Honestly, I don't think people should be allowed to get married without proper training, testing, and earning of a certificate of completion. After all, you have to be educated and tested on everything else you need a license for – why is marriage treated differently? The powers that be should think about that.

As it turns out, my husband was secretly seeing a psychologist.

Being a farmer, I'm guessing he was home most of the day, so he always collected and previewed our mail. One day I beat him to it and discovered a statement from a doctor's office. Naturally, he never mentioned that he was seeing a doctor, so I asked him about it. I had no clue what was going on in his life, and he preferred it that way. Preposterous! I simply could not understand why he wouldn't tell me anything. After all, I was his wife not a stranger, and I wanted to know what was going on. Surprisingly, he shared with me something he had been experiencing for months and months, completely unbeknownst to me. He assumed I wouldn't understand and scheduled a session for me with his doctor so that I could learn about what he was going through. Brilliant. And I'll never forget that meeting.

My husband was having panic attacks. Some days he felt paralyzed by too much responsibility and couldn't decide what to do first, so he did nothing and sat in his chair all day. He wasn't eating properly, wasn't sleeping well, and often felt like he was stranded in the middle of the field having a heart attack and was unable to call for help. His symptoms were frustrating, depressing, scary, and felt life-threatening. What was causing this?

After his doctor explained this to me, she asked, "What do you think is going on in your marriage?"

I stated, "Basically, we don't get along, we don't talk, and we don't spend time together. He is cold and mean-spirited, enjoys berating me, insulting me, and ignoring me. This is not my idea of a marriage, and we need counseling to make things better between us."

She replied, "He cannot go through marriage counseling while he is being treated by me, as it would be too much for him to handle."

"Well, just what am I supposed to do then?"

"Detach yourself from him emotionally. He doesn't mean what he's saying to you right now. If you love him, be patient, and be there for him if he wants you. Stay away from him if that's what he needs from you."

Huh? What kind of advice is that for newlyweds? I was sad, angry, confused, crying and, of course, thinking about myself and what I wanted out of life. Get a grip!

I asked, "What about me? How long am I supposed to do this?"

She said, "As long as it takes. You married him for better or for worse, in sickness and in health. If he were lying in a hospital bed suffering from cancer, you would understand because you could see it. But because his problem is in his mind, you can't physically see him suffering, so it doesn't make sense to you."

Well heavenly days, make me feel like a horrible, selfish wench. So, OK then. I stopped crying, put on my tough girl face, and decided to do what she said. I went home and detached myself emotionally from my husband. He could ignore me, scream insults at me, even point a gun at me — it no longer mattered. I became emotionally detached. And then I stopped caring. I don't think that's what she meant for me to do, but that's what happened.

Was this her evil deed or mine? For a professional counselor, I still believe her advice was extremely harsh, and she could have done far more to help us than to turn us loose with a statement like that. Was I still being selfish -- not understanding what he was going through and not trying to help him? But what could I do? At her suggestion, I left him alone, I stopped asking questions, and I had no expectations. I lived my own, solitary, busy life.

Another year went by and I saw no change - no improvement whatsoever. One night in December of 1992, we actually sat down at the kitchen table and talked about it.

He told me, "You are emotionally immature, read too many romance novels, and live in a fantasy world, which is why you will never be happy. An adult should never be dependent on another adult for emotional support, and this is a sickness you have that will prevent you from ever functioning in reality."

At least that's how I remember it. What a ridiculous statement! And by that time, we had seen two different marriage counselors (against the sage advice of his brilliant psychologist) and the last one told me our fate was obvious. Our "marriage" was over. That was in 1993, and the scars are permanent, although they do fade. However, some things you just don't forget.

Chapter 4

"Things may not be great – but you are!"
Card from Aunt Phyllis

I had never had a CT scan before, but I was about to see what the fuss was all about. The point was to determine where in my body the disease was located.

Ushered into a locker room with several other patients, the nurse presented each of us with two lovely green gowns and a pair of socks.

"Step into the changing booth and undress, except for your underwear. Put your things in a locker and go to the waiting room."

For modesty, you put one gown on forward and the other on backward and tie them closed by yourself. With that they think I should feel adequately covered? Please. I shuffled into the chilly waiting room where they gave me two jugs of barium solution to drink over a period of time. It didn't taste that bad and was no big deal. The nurse graciously handed me a warm blanket so I wouldn't freeze to death while I waited. I quickly crawled under the blanket, tucked my legs underneath me, read a magazine to pass the time and listened to some of the conversation around me.

Two older ladies were talking about this being their second CT scan. They had been experiencing nausea and tingling fingertips throughout their treatments. They both looked completely normal, not sickly, exhausted or miserable, which was good news to me. They both still had nice hair. When they started talking about their hair, I learned they were wearing wigs. Really?! I tried not to stare, but one in particular was salt and pepper and looked unbelievably natural. That was good news, too, although it is possible I won't lose my hair. I just can't imagine what that would be like, as I have always had a full head of thick hair. Time will tell. I'm sure there is a wig shopping trip in my near future. I can have long hair, short hair, red hair, blonde hair … whatever I want. Could be fun!

A technician called me into an even colder scanning room, laid me out on the table, covered me with another blanket, and ran the tests. I didn't feel anything, just closed my eyes and rested. I wasn't nervous, I didn't cry, I was just fine. Now I have to wait for the results.

Divorce

Wait, wait, wait. I'm not a particularly patient person, but at my advanced age, I have learned how to wait. Years ago, I waited to get married. Then I waited for my husband to share his life with me, but all I could do was observe in amazement.

We lived in an old, two-story white farm house in the country. I woke up in the middle of the night once and realized I was still in bed alone. I walked quietly down the stairs and peeked around the corner to see what on earth he could be doing. He was in the living room sitting on the floor watching TV, chewing tobacco (gross!) and cleaning guns. Another time in the middle of the night, he was outside digging weeds by flashlight. Good grief – we had neighbors. Did they ever notice his odd schedule or behavior? For numerous reasons, he felt compelled to stay awake all night. I never understood how he could keep those hours, and it certainly isn't the way I assumed he lived his life prior to marrying me. No early to bed, early to rise for this farmer! Who knew?

I learned that part of the reason he stayed up all night was because he could not fall asleep until I was asleep, as he had a bed to himself up to that point in his life. So, I never saw him get ready for bed. One day as I was making our waterbed, I noticed the bottom of the bed was all wet – not by the drain, so I knew it wasn't leaking.

I asked, "Why are the sheets wet?"

Much to my surprise, he actually launched into an explanation. "I like to sleep on my back with my knees up, but with the satin sheets you insist on using, my feet slip and won't stay in place, and I can't sleep. So, I have to put on socks, wet them down in the bathtub, walk up the stairs on the sides of my feet, and plant wet socks on the sheets. Then I can fall asleep."

Ha! I had no idea! Poor goofy fella.

He was also goofy enough not to follow the Rules of Common Courtesy, and we had an ongoing battle with putting things away.

1. When you're finished with the milk, put it back in the refrigerator – do not leave it on the counter.

2. When you're finished in the cupboard, close the cabinet door.

3. When you're finished with the hair dryer, put it away.

Did he go to kindergarten? Like a child, he refused to do these things, especially after I asked him to do it. It's not like he was so busy that he didn't have time to pick up after himself, he just never had to do it before so I suppose these things never crossed his mind. How is that even possible? Since he lived with his parents until the day we got married, his mom took care of everything. Her house was perfect. However, some days I would come home from work and it looked like a tornado had ripped through our house. To show him how it annoyed me, every time he left the hair dryer out, I would unplug it and leave it in the middle of the bathroom floor so he had to step over it or trip on it. Sometimes he would pick it up; sometimes he wouldn't. He would leave his mail piled on the kitchen table for weeks at a time until I took it upstairs and threw it in his office. How hard is it??!! We had a battle of wills, that's for sure.

I enjoyed cooking, but he was not interested in eating what I made. The morning after we got home from our honeymoon, I got up early and made breakfast for us. He said he didn't have time to eat and left. That was my last attempt at making breakfast for him. When I got home from work that night, I made a spaghetti dinner. He didn't want spaghetti and wouldn't eat it. I was mad and confused. He would rather eat frozen egg rolls or Army c-rations for weeks than anything I ever made, and I can cook! So … I was destined to eat alone and let him fend for himself. This lifestyle was just not normal and was certainly not how I wanted to grow old.

My saving grace was his Grandmother, whom I adored. She knew things were not great between us and that I was sad, lonely and unhappy but didn't know what to do about it. I married him for better, for worse, in sickness and in health, and I believed in my vows and she knew that.

One day she pulled me aside and said, "You may have made your bed, but you don't have to sleep in it."

She had just given me her blessing and the gift of new life without guilt. As far as I was concerned, she had given me permission to go and the marriage counselors confirmed that I had done all I could. OK then -- no more waiting; I'm out of here.

Chapter 5

*"Special K – Just thought you could use
a little extra sunshine today!"*

Card from friend Daniel T.

After work the next afternoon, my lovely and generous boss took my teammate from the office and me to a salon on Oak Street to get haircuts. I had long straight hair, which I loved, but was ready for a change. Since the chances of it falling out during chemotherapy were high, we decided that I might as well enjoy a new look for a few weeks and maybe even buy a wig in this new style. Wouldn't that be fun?! I showed the stylist a picture from a magazine that I thought would be cute – she agreed. So after I settled into the chair with a freshly shampooed head, we pulled my hair into a ponytail and whacked off 10 inches … just like that … clip … gone. I didn't feel anything. No pain, no sense of loss, no tears. I was ready for shorter hair. She handed my ponytail to me for safekeeping, as I had plans to mail it to "Locks of Love" for those who can't grow hair. I'm fortunate; mine *will* grow back.

She cut and styled for a while and all of a sudden I had a new look. Wow! We all just loved it. And I'm not just saying that – I looked 10 years younger and had a sleek, sophisticated style that brought out the auburn in my hair, the color in my face, and the blue of my eyes. Not sure I would ever be able to duplicate the style, but I'd sure give it a try. I thought, "Guess I won't wash my hair for a few days and enjoy this. Ha!"

My teammate was next and also got a darling cut straight from a magazine. She's a young gal with perfect skin and a gorgeous face, so she didn't have as drastic a change as I did, and she looked radiant. We went to a new bar nearby to celebrate with a few cocktails. Nobody so much as gave me a second glance, so maybe my change wasn't all THAT dramatic. Rats. Oh well, I loved it!

Boyfriend #1

Getting divorced was a dramatic change. I loved being on my own and truth be told, my ex loved it, too. In fact, he stayed in touch with me by telephone for a few months and actually thanked me for leaving, even though he hated me at first. Amazingly, I still felt nothing, as I had truly detached myself from him emotionally. He once told me that I had wasted 11 years of his life. Is that so? That was 11 years of my childbearing years, too, you ying-yang. But whatever – at least he was saying something.

Being on his own apparently freed him from the stuck-at-home trap, as he renewed his relationship with his brother and began enjoying a social life. During our marriage, there was no time for a vacation. He was much too busy (doing WHAT I never knew.) However, that summer I learned he flew to Jamaica with his new girlfriend, his brother and a group of their friends. How do you like that?! I was seriously annoyed when I heard it and would have enjoyed giving him a piece of my mind, but of course I never did. I also heard he was obnoxiously drunk on the plane and behaved horribly, and I was super glad I didn't have to endure it. Not my problem.

However, my problem quickly turned into my first boyfriend. My ex was the only man I had been with sexually, and I was petrified to open that door with someone else. Five months after our dissolution, a girlfriend of mine introduced me to a guy who played softball with her husband. He was tall, athletic, a whopping 41 years old, and had the guy-next-door looks that grow on you – at least they grew on me. He seemed confident, yet shy, and I was intrigued. He was a tri-athlete who had recently gotten the Triathlon logo tattooed on his shoulder blade – sexy! Who would go through the pain of getting a tattoo??! I didn't understand that, but I did think it looked pretty cool.

Having been fairly sheltered and remaining a little (OK – a lot) naïve, I finally decided I was going to spend some quality time with this guy. Yipes, I had no idea what I was doing! We went out a few times during which I gained self-confidence and decided he was trustworthy. Eventually, kissing led to getting naked which led to sex – just like that. I was shocked and surprised at how easy it was and how comfortable we were. Who would have thought I suffered through all that anxiety just worrying about the possibility? Shortly thereafter, he asked for a key to my apartment so he could come over and be waiting for me when I got home from work – how different and how sweet!

One day at work, a co-worker's darling son came into the office. Hottie! He chatted me up and asked for my phone number. How flattering and exciting! Should I give it to him? I had a new boyfriend after all. What the heck -- I'd give him my number and see if he would call. Suddenly, I was wracked with guilt and sick to my stomach – and I'm not Catholic or Jewish, but a good, solid Methodist. But it didn't feel like the right thing to do and I couldn't take it back – he had left the building. What to do? What to do? I went home and there was my boyfriend waiting for me. He knew right away by the look on my face that something was wrong. Apparently, I'm like an open book. I had no intention of telling him anything. However, after a few direct questions, I confessed.

"I gave my number to another guy today. I feel just sick about it, and I probably won't ever see him anyway. I'm sorry, I shouldn't have done it. No big deal, right?"

Well, Mr. Triathlon was not happy. His smile disappeared and a chill filled the room as he stood up and walked toward me. Gulp.

In an icy tone, he said, "You're newly divorced and not even 30 years old. You obviously need to date other people."

He tossed my key on the table and declared flatly, "Don't call me."

Out the door he flew! Wow. I stood there in stunned silence – surprised, devastated, and heartbroken – but I let him go, as I didn't know what else to do. It was my fault, and I truly felt horrible.

Later that night, I couldn't sleep and couldn't stand that he left mad at me, so I went to his apartment. Much to my dismay, I quickly learned that my boyfriend was so upset that he fell into the arms of a good-old standby booty-call girlfriend and really didn't want to see me again. Huh? Just like that? I'm so sure! I was livid – how could he do this to me? Evil!! I didn't even do anything other than give out my number and be honest about it.

BIG lesson. In the future, do NOT tell. Ha! Or is the lesson, do NOT give out your phone number when you're dating someone? Boyfriend #1 fired me. And the nerve of the little hottie who took my number – he never even bothered to call! Bastard. What's that about? Who makes the rules anyway? I haven't been in the dating scene for 11 years, so I guess it would behoove me to figure out how it works.

In the end, I guess it was just a blessing in disguise. Within the next few months, Mr. Triathlon impregnated one of his co-workers, married her, and the last newsflash I heard, they had three meek children. Interesting how things have a way of working themselves out.

Chapter 6

*"Some people love others and are always prepared to stop,
lend a helping hand.
They bring real sunshine into the lives of others."*
Card from Gram Reese

Another week later, on October 20, 2005, I had the first consultation with my Hematologist and his nurse practitioner to review my biopsy, diagnosis and planned treatment. Yipes! What are they going to tell me? Is this going to hurt? Am I going to be sick? Am I going to be able to work? Am I going to be able to continue working out? Is all my hair going to fall out? Is my skin going to shrivel up, dry out, and be covered with oozing sores and scabs? Am I going to get painful, swollen mouth sores? Are my fingernails going to turn black, thin out, split and chip? Am I going to have to change my eating habits? Am I going to lose weight? Gain weight? Am I going to lose my fertility?! So many questions, I honestly don't know what to expect. I'm very worried about what's going to happen to me, but how bad can it be? I feel fine. I'm not going to die, after all. Right?

Thankfully, Stephanie went with me, as we both knew my mind would not be able to absorb all the information. I was still shocked that this was actually happening to me. I sat through their explanations as bravely as possible doing my best to stay dry-eyed and nonchalant about how this disease was going to change my life. It's so hard to listen and pay attention. What did they say?

First, it is confirmed that I have been diagnosed with Lymphocyte Rich Hodgkin's Lymphoma, and I didn't do anything wrong to get it. (I guess that's a relief.) I think this is when they told me the CT Scan revealed that the disease is in my neck, under my arms, in my chest, only on one side of my diaphragm, and not in any of my organs. (This

27

is actually good news!) The doctor estimates that I am in Stage II, but can't be certain until we run some additional tests. I'm thankful that so far it seems we have caught this fairly early, which must mean that treatment will be less harsh.

Second, now that the diagnosis has been confirmed, the disease needs to be staged.

"Staging (the process of determining how far the cancer has spread) is necessary for a physician to plan treatment. The lower the stage, the earlier the disease has been identified and the better the prognosis for recovery." (cancer.healthcenteronline.com)

In order to determine the stage, I will need a PET Scan, Bone Marrow Biopsy, additional blood work, heart and lung tests. OK, that doesn't sound so bad. Besides, I can't imagine that the disease has advanced very far … I haven't felt sick for even a moment, I haven't lost a single pound, and I'm not tired. Thank God I found a huge lump on my neck so at least I knew something was up!

Third, the main methods used to treat Hodgkin's lymphoma are chemotherapy, radiation therapy and high-dose chemotherapy with blood restoring stem cell transplants.

As I'm trying to listen and understand this information, my heart is pounding and I'm starting to sweat (don't cry, don't cry) … this sounds positively dreadful. What is all of this going to do to me? Exactly where did this come from? I have no idea, and I just hate that this is happening. Why, why, why me?

Fortunately, they say I will only need chemotherapy (drugs) to attack my cancerous cells – no radiation. The way I understand it, we have cells in our bodies that grow and die every day. When they grow but don't die, they collect, become tumors, and create all kinds of problems. It's amazing what goes on in our bodies that the average person knows nothing about!

The drugs will be administered directly into my veins through an IV – I won't need a shunt put into my arm or chest – more good news as those can have enough foul problems of their own. They will simply insert the IV before each of my treatments, which will be every two weeks for four to six months. That's a LOT of sticking – good thing I have big, strong veins. Since the disease is in multiple nodes, I will not be getting radiation treatments. I'm very happy to hear that because I've heard horror stories about radiation, what it does to you, and how it makes you feel. My heart aches for people who have to do both.

My treatment regime is made up of four drugs. These can be some of the problems associated with each:

A = Adriamycin (hair loss, nausea, fatigue, heart problems in older people)

B = Bleomycin (lung toxicity, may cause fever)

V = Velban (numbness, tingling in fingers and toes, constipation, nausea, fatigue)

D = Dacarbazine (achey, flu-like symptoms, nausea, fatigue)

Every morning, I am to take a birth control pill (no period until this is all over!), one Ativan to prevent nausea, one Diflucan to prevent mouth sores, and 3 times a week, one Bactrim-DS that is an antibiotic since I will have a very low white blood cell count. I should take my daily vitamin every day except the day before, day of and day after a treatment. I am supposed to drink a lot of water and juice and enjoy something chocolate every single day. The chocolate is my own regimen – gotta have it for my disposition!

Sounds like I can pretty much expect to be nauseous and exhausted for the next six months of my life. However, they will shoot me with anti-nausea medicine before injecting these drugs to help prevent the nausea. Makes me feel sick just thinking about it. I hate throwing up. When I was a child, I used to throw up whenever I ate spaghetti. Mom said it was because I swallowed it without chewing, apparently because I'm lazy or something crazy like that. When I got to clean up the mess, believe me, I learned how to chew. Please, please, please let this medicine work for me. I don't know how I'm going to be able to stand this. I am very rarely sick, and I enjoy being healthy and active. I plan to stay that way.

A review of my PET Scan showed a spot on my lung. The doctor didn't really think it was Hodgkin's, but we won't know for certain until after the treatments. It's probably just scar tissue from bronchitis. I'm going to believe that's what it is anyway and nothing I'm going to worry about now. After four cycles of treatments, they will repeat the PET Scan, CT Scan, heart and lung tests to see if the disease is gone. If it is gone, I get two more cycles for good measure. If it is not gone, I get four more cycles. At least now I know the time frame.

If I develop a temperature of 99.9, I am not supposed to take Tylenol as it might mask a problem. If I get a fever of 101 or higher, I am supposed to call my nurse practitioner and go to the emergency room. I don't have a big desire to sit and wait for hours in the emergency room, but I am supposed to go if I have uncontrolled nausea/vomiting/diarrhea, pain or burning with urination, or if I develop sores in my mouth. I'd rather club myself in the head than suffer through an evening in the ER.

Magazine Man

Every time I run into "Magazine Man," I get a mental club to the head. The spring before I moved to Chicago (1994), my Grandpa passed away. While visiting Grandma, I read a woman's magazine that featured three handsome, single men — one from Chicago! The article suggested I write to him ... so I did. And I kept his picture on my desk for the next three months so I could gaze at him and read his profile over and over ... he had become part of my daily life. He gave me hope for a future in Chicago with a handsome, successful entrepreneur whose path I merely needed to cross. However, he never wrote me back. The nerve! So when I packed up my bags preparing for Big City life, Magazine Man was tossed into the garbage with all the other clutter I was not taking with me. Time for a fresh start!

About two months later (on my Grandma's birthday no less!), I was at a bar in the Gold Coast with a girlfriend enjoying a Thursday night out on the town. From where I was standing, I could see the front door. Much to my amazement, in sauntered Magazine Man and two of his friends. I could not believe my eyes! He looked exactly like his picture. Seriously, exactly the same: crisp white shirt under a green vest, dazzling white perfect teeth smile, side-part dark wavy hair, sparkling eyes, square jaw ... there was no mistaking it was him in the flesh! What were the chances of that happening after being in Chicago for only two months? The Universe was on my side, and I was so lucky!! Our paths had actually crossed!

I stopped this gorgeous man in his tracks, introduced myself, and told him how I knew who he was. Surprised and embarrassed, he explained that the whole magazine article was just a fluke his friends had talked him into doing. He played along like he remembered my letter, but later admitted getting hundreds of them and didn't respond to any. We laughed and laughed, introduced our friends, and exchanged numbers by the end of the night. I was floating on clouds! He was beautiful, funny, and just as charming as I had imagined.

Two days later, he called and asked me out for dinner. Barely taking time to hang up the phone, I leapt around the room squealing with delight and hugging my roommate ... I was beyond excited!! My first Chicago date and with Magazine Man of all people!! We had agreed to meet at an Italian restaurant not far from my neighborhood. That evening, I took the train from work and marched quickly so I would not be late. He was waiting for me, and I couldn't have been more pleased to be sharing the evening with this handsome dream come true. We exchanged stories and jokes, ate yummy Italian food, drank wine, and had a lovely time. My nerves had calmed as I realized he was a real person, a true Chicago bachelor, and then he offered to drive me home.

Panic struck, and I thought, "Oh boy, this could be a serious problem."

How am I going to give him directions to my apartment? I had just moved to this confusing city, and I had one path to and from work. I had no idea how to get home! I knew my address but which way was north? Or east? OK, the lake is east, but I don't see the lake! I know up from down, but that's about it. East-West, North-South – beats me! He's lived here forever, he should know how to find my address – I have no clue. But I'm a cool, savvy, city gal now – I'll find it. Can't let on that I don't know how to get home. After all, I had just spent the last two hours being charming, witty and intelligent.

As we walked to a parking lot down the street, I wondered what kind of vehicle he drove … SUV, sedan, or sports car … but of course I would never ask. He must have sensed my thoughts churning, as he played the game of letting me survey the cars and walk to the one I assumed must be his. With a look of pride and joy, he unlocked the doors of an expensive looking little red sports car.

"How cute!" I exclaimed.

He gave me a shattered look that silently declared, "No, you country bumpkin, this is NOT a cute car. It is fast, hot and sexy, not cute." Oops – I was not scoring points for sophistication. I should have just kept my mouth shut. He never said a word as he opened the door for me, but his body language and facial expression clearly said he was not amused by my exclamation.

Now we were faced with the challenge of getting me home. I had to confess that I didn't quite know which direction to go, but I could recite my address! Surely he knew enough about the city to find it with my address. *Apparently not.* Once again, he was not amused, and I was horribly embarrassed by my lack of directional sense.

As we drove around searching for my apartment, he grew increasingly annoyed.

"Sorry, this is off my path!" He rolled his eyes and huffed in response. Where was his sense of adventure? After all, this was more quality time for us to get to know each other, but I didn't bring that up.

I had no idea where we were, and I was feeling more and more stressed, stupid and helpless with each passing moment. Of course, that was back in the days before cell phones and GPS, so I couldn't get any help. Finally, we managed to find my home. What a relief. I couldn't leap out of the car fast enough ... oh well.

Much to my surprise and delight, he called me the next day! Perhaps he would allow me an opportunity to redeem myself. As it turns out, we talked on the phone every now and then but didn't get together for another month. One Monday night, he and a friend met me and my friends at a bar to watch "Melrose Place." They walked us home afterwards, but it was very awkward and uncomfortable. I realized then that he wasn't all that, and we just didn't have much in common.

We never got together again, but I still run into him about once a year in the Gold Coast. We always give a hug hello and enjoy a secret chuckle over how we met — a story neither of us will ever forget! We are both still single, live in the city, and love to travel, but I feel like he always views me as a young, naïve girl from the country — not one of the sophisticated, edgy, city women he dates.

Too bad ... his loss. He wasn't evil, just self-absorbed and enjoying the Chicago playground. By golly, I'm going to enjoy it, too!

Chapter 7

"You are always living life to the fullest and are so intelligent, independent, beautiful and caring. You've really shown me, whether you realize it or not, that you can achieve anything you put your mind to."

Handwritten by friend Leah

Wednesday, October 26, 2005. The time has come for all the testing to determine the stage of my disease. I actually feel badly for the staff at the hospital because I am crabby and not in the mood to sit around all day. As long as I show up on time for my appointments, I should be able to put on my scowl face and nobody should talk to me more than necessary. For Stephanie's benefit, I will be as cheerful as possible. She is here for the first procedure and then will go to work. I'm a little scared and nervous because I don't know what to expect, but I am curious to see how this whole process works.

Looking around, I don't really see any young people here. Most of the patients are older, have someone waiting with them, and really don't look like they feel well. They don't want to talk or be bothered either. It is sad and depressing, yet again makes me feel lucky and fortunate that I'm going to breeze through this and bounce back quickly. How do people work here and deal with all of this sickness and sadness? Thank God they do. My first year of college was in nursing school. What was I thinking?! I should have been a candy striper for a summer, then I would have known that the duties of a nurse were not my bag! I truly admire everyone who works in healthcare. I simply don't have the stomach for it.

Since my chest x-rays were done during last week's visit, today I start with a bone marrow biopsy. I'm told it is uncomfortable, but not painful like a spinal tap – whatever that means. They don't ask me to change into a paper gown, so I can wear my own clothes. That's surprising and interesting – so how bad can it be?

We are led through the maze of hallways into an exam room. The nurse practitioner, who is getting to know me pretty well by now, asks me to unbutton my jeans and lie down on the table, face down. If anyone else asked me to do that, I'd have to protest! However, I'm starting to feel nervous, trying to remain calm, and will keep my joke to myself. What is she going to do? Stephanie sits in a chair next to me with the newest gossip magazines to read and shows me pictures so I'll be distracted from the procedure. As soon as she said, "Don't look at the tray," and started flipping through the magazine to distract me, my heart began pounding and I couldn't focus, but I would do my best to look at pictures of all the healthy, glamorous stars. Stephanie is a champ – what would I do without her?!! So I don't look at the tray, and my eyes move from her face to the magazine.

The nurse cleans off a patch of skin on both sides of my pelvic bone. She explains that she will be giving me a local anesthetic so that a small incision can be made for the needles to enter to get samples of bone marrow and bone tissue. That's fine – ok. The shots are done, the incisions made – no problem, I barely felt it, and I'm learning about the latest Hollywood news. Next, she said I would feel a slight vacuum sensation as she extracts the bone marrow. YEOWZA!! I do not feel a SLIGHT anything; I feel an intense shooting pain go up my back.

"STOP, I can feel that!"

The nurse gave me another painkiller shot. OK, I will try not to move this time. I have a death grip on the table, I'm sweating bullets, and the tears are flowing and soaking the paper under my head. This is so scary and unfair. I hate it. She asked if she should stop again.

"No, just get it over with fast."

Stephanie fans me with her magazine trying to cool me down and asks if I'm ok. My eyes are shut tight, and I can't help that the tears are flowing, but I nod my head yes and swallow hard. But I'm really thinking, "No, I'm not ok! Cripes, I'm being stabbed and my bone marrow is being sucked out ... this is not easy or painless -- it's horrible!" Finally, she's done. I relax my grip on the table, breathe a huge sigh of relief, blow my nose, and wipe my face.

Then the nurse said, "OK, now we have to do the other side." Huh?! Oh, my dear God. Fine – just do it. At least I know what to expect now. The repeat performance on the other side was equally as horrible. I'm wiped out – thankfully that is over.

The nurse announced, "OK, now we have to extract some bone." WHAT?! I thought we were done, but that was just the marrow. Goody. I lie back down on my tear soaked protective paper and grip the table while Stephanie does her best to fan me, as she knows I'm about to break into another sweat.

The nurse attempts to insert the needle into my pelvic bone and asks, "Do you work out?"

"Yes, why?"

"Your bones are very hard – this is going to make it harder on both of us." She jams the needle in once, but didn't get enough of a sample. She goes back in for a second try. The other side gets a good sample on the first try. This procedure was dreadful as well, but not as shocking as the first one. I'm going to survive. The nurse bandages up my incisions – no stitches. Hooray – we're done here.

I try to stand up but feel a little dizzy and disoriented and my eyes feel swollen. I'm tired. How do old people and children endure this? The nurse said the three anesthetic shots she gave me might make it difficult to walk, but I seem fine other than having trouble focusing. I feel like I just slept for 12 hours on my face.

Again, Stephanie said, "Don't look at the tray." Naturally, I looked. Beside the big, bad needles, there are now smears of my blood and bone. That doesn't bother me – in fact, it's fascinating. My prayer is that they don't find any disease in either of them.

Stephanie has to leave for work, so I'll be on my own for the balance of the day. I'm sure it's not easy for her to watch me go through this. She has gone through plenty of medical procedures without even telling me about it until afterwards. I certainly would have been there for her had I known.

I made the mistake of wearing jeans today. Nobody told me to wear comfy pants. Now I will have these huge bandages rubbing against my back the rest of the day. Somebody should have told me I wasn't spending the day in a lovely green hospital gown, and I would have dressed more comfortably. I wish I could just lie down and go to sleep, but I have to go wait in line for the Muga Scan (heart test). Fortunately, no treadmill or exercise of any kind is involved in this test or the PET Scan to follow. I can just sit in the waiting room and wait, which is pretty much what I will do for the rest of the day. I will either be sitting and waiting or horizontal in a tube getting scanned. What a long, long exhausting day, but it is best to get these tests all over with at once.

Lazy Boy

All the waiting around gave me plenty of time to think. How much heartache and disappointment can one girl take in a lifetime? Shortly after seeing Magazine Man for the last time, I met a tall cutie patootie at a late night dance club. We had great fun for a couple of weeks hanging out, drinking, dancing, and cavorting. Then he started calling me at work every morning while he was at home lying in bed, not working. He thought it was endearing that he thought of me when he woke up in the middle of the day. Hm. My heart was not growing fonder. In fact, as he continued to call me from his bed every day, I grew increasingly annoyed and realized that I could never date somebody who was at home sleeping while I was at work. Made me crazy. Every time the caller ID showed his number, I rolled my eyes and let him go into voice mail. What an ingenious invention! But that's also when I knew it was time -- I had to let him go. He wasn't evil by any means, just lazy. Lazy doesn't work for me. Next!

Chapter 8

"Thinking of you and praying that God will give you
A day filled with comfort and special blessings."
Card from Aunt Pam and Uncle Chuck

Two days later, I was back in the hospital for a Pulmonary Function test for which they had slotted two hours. I've never been fond of blowing up balloons, as it strains the little part of my neck under my ear and feels like my eardrums will burst. Maybe I don't do it right. Anyway, this test was similar to blowing up a balloon, except I had to shove a big plastic hose in my mouth and blow into it over and over and over. Apparently, I wasn't doing it right because I had to keep doing it again and again. How am I going to do this for two hours? Give me a break! I had to sit in a little booth to do this and could see my reflection in the plexiglass with my lips tightly stretched over a monstrous tube, drool spilling out the corners of my mouth, my eyes rolling up in my head in annoyance ... I am not enjoying this. The tech says, "Take a big, deep breath and blow, blow, blow ... faster, harder, until every last bit of air is out of your lungs. (pause) Now, do it again."

As if this weren't humiliating enough, she left the door to the room wide open and naturally, every person walking by looked in to watch. Rude! Why didn't I ask her to close the door? Dumb. Fortunately for me, two hours was a gross exaggeration, as the tests only took about 15 minutes of my life, and then I was free to go – never knowing who watched me that afternoon.

Funny Guy

I have to say, this reminds me of a significantly horrible experience my roommate and I had shortly after Lazy Boy got the boot. We went out to a trendy saloon (as my boss at the time was fond of calling bars) where we ran into a guy my roomie knew from college. His friend looked like a frightening combination of my ex-husband and Jerry Seinfeld. Being the great wing-gal that I was, I decided to make the most of the situation and see what this guy was like. He was entertaining, slightly amusing, and arrogant. Several hours and numerous drinks later when he was really funny and very handsome, we stumbled to their apartment. Music was turned on loudly, lights were switched off, candles were set ablaze, and before I realized it, I was faced with another Pulmonary Function test. What the hell?! I was suddenly able to think ... what on earth am I doing and where is my roommate? As I snapped out of it, stood up and adjusted my vision, I noticed College Boy leaning on the doorway, arms and ankles crossed, amused smirk on his nasty face, watching me. Evil!

I was beyond mortified, but don't recall saying a word – I just wanted to get the heck out of dodge! Those two pricks got a huge guffaw out of the little show – I was not even slightly amused and if looks could kill ... both of them would have gone up in flames at that very moment. As it was, they stood by and watched me as I snapped up my shirt from the floor and stomped around in search of my roommate – I found her passed out in a bedroom. I will not say what she told me happened in there, but believe me, those two idiots enjoyed sharing the evening's adventures with their buddies. I know this because the following weekend, we were at one of our favorite saloons and had the misfortune of running into College Boy, Funny Guy and a gaggle of their idiot cronies. They pointed at us, whispered amongst themselves, then hooted and hollered ... EVIL!

My roomie and I stood transfixed in shock and disbelief for what felt like an eternity, then looked each other in the eye, and with an unspoken agreement, bolted out the door at lightning speed. We couldn't get away from the horror we felt, and of course, analyzed the situation for the rest of the evening. My poor roommate was in tears for a week, and I was livid and embarrassed. Unbelievable!

Truly, we were naïve, careless and allowed ourselves to be in that situation, but those fools were mean-spirited and pure evil. Turns out, we never saw them again. Lucky, lucky on so many levels!

Chapter 9

"Wishing you happier and healthier days ahead –
You will get there!"
Card from Friends Pam & Dave

The weekend after all the staging tests were completed happened to be my mom's birthday, so Stephanie and I were going home for a visit and telling the family about my ugly news. I had thought and thought about how to tell them ... what to say, how to put a positive spin on it, show no fear because I am brave, strong and very rarely sick ... but just thinking about telling them brought tears to my eyes and made me feel terrible -- hot, sweaty, nervous, sad, guilty, brain dead. I have no idea what to say or how to say it, and I know I can't do it. Stephanie is going to have to do it – yep, she can do it for me. I just have to ask her.

Turns out, I didn't have to ask her. In the car on our 2-1/2 hour trip south, when I brought up telling them she said, "You won't be able to tell them. I will." Whew, what a relief – she knows me so well. And she will handle it very matter of factly and without emotion. I have been diagnosed with a cancer called Hodgkin's Lymphoma – I didn't do anything to get it, I will have the best doctors in the city caring for me, and the disease responds very well to treatment. That's all we really know. It is what it is. Let's deal with it.

When we arrived at the farm, we both did our best to act as if everything was completely normal. The dogs came bounding out to meet us, the chickens (Hillary, Jody and Theresa) clucked a greeting, the cats ignored us, and the Kettles (as Stephanie affectionately nicknamed our parents) came out to see if we needed help carrying in our bags. We settled in, had a snack, and caught up on the latest. That evening, a girlfriend of mine from high school came over to watch a movie and play cards. That was a little unusual, but I had already told her about the cancer, so she wanted to see me but promised not to say anything. Her son was the 3-year old ring bearer in my wedding, and I really feel my age when she tells me he is a senior in high school preparing to start college in the fall. Huh? How is that possible?! I haven't even had a baby yet ... I better get on with the program! Makes me very sad to think I may never have a family of my own ... well, I have other things to concentrate on right now. First things first.

I thought Stephanie might take the opportunity Saturday night to share the news, but she didn't. So as usual, Sunday morning we got up, went for a walk, attended worship service, and went back home for lunch. Our brother, Tim, called to say he had been asked out for lunch by friends, but Stephanie was insistent that he come home and have lunch with us. For crying out loud, how often do we see him anyway – once every three months at best – he can come home and have lunch with us. The Kettles thought it was a little strange that she insisted on him joining us because it has never been an issue before, but they weren't going to cross her – she seemed a little crabby. Only I knew how much pressure she was feeling and why. I felt terrible putting the burden on her. I also know she handles stress with anger while I shed tears. I felt nervous waiting and wondering when she was going to speak up. Tick, Tock ... our visit was almost over, as we usually leave shortly after lunch.

After we ate lunch, had dessert and cleaned the kitchen ... nobody scattered ... we all just sat around the table as if we were waiting for something to happen. I looked at Stephanie with big eyes like ... hello ... what are you waiting for??!! Just when I thought I would tell them myself, she began. With the first words out of her mouth (I'm not even sure what they were), I put my head down, closed my eyes, rubbed my lips together, and folded my hands in my lap. My face wrinkled up, my nose tingled, my body started sweating, my heart was aching, and my tears started dripping onto my hands. Was I breathing? I couldn't look at anyone. I couldn't listen to or absorb anything she was saying. My ears were ringing and my head was throbbing. I felt absolutely devastated and helpless, as if I were hurting my family by telling them that I had cancer. Am I letting them down? I definitely don't want them to feel sorry for me, and I certainly don't want to see pity or compassion in their eyes. I don't know what I want from them, and I don't expect anything from them. They are my family – they are all I have. I just want them to know.

While we all love each other very much, we certainly don't say so and the extent of our emotional support is usually in the form of a quick hug. I dared to look up, as I wanted to know if anyone had a reaction to this horrific news. Stephanie was strong and solid, I believe my dad was asking a few questions, Tim was just taking it in, and mom was crying. She got out of her chair, came over and gave me a real, honest, heartfelt hug that sent me into sobs. She was so sorry. That's all anyone can say really – I'm so sorry you're going through this. Of course, when you hear someone has cancer, your thoughts turn to pain, suffering, and death – all horrible and heartbreaking. I'm so sorry is just about all you can say because you can't fix it.

They became curious. How did I know I had a problem? Was I sick? What happened?

This summer, the day after my birthday in fact, I was taking a shower and noticed my right armpit hurt as if I had lifted too many weights at the gym the night before. Since I didn't go to the gym the night before, that was not even possible. Poking around, I found the source of my pain – a swollen lymph gland. Hm. No big deal – I must be fighting something. I'll pay attention to it for a few days until it goes away. Three days later, the lump was still there, but it didn't hurt anymore. However, my hand grazed the right side of my neck while I was getting ready for work, and I felt a huge lump. What is this?! Hm. A lump under my arm and now in my neck. It's hard, doesn't hurt, but it is huge! This is not normal and can't be good. I better do something. I called an internist that day to check it out.

I didn't panic or freak out. While I couldn't imagine what it could be, I knew it shouldn't be ignored. Besides, how bad could it be? The lumps surely haven't been there very long. After all, I wasn't feeling sick or tired, didn't have any unexplained weight loss, nothing was going on … I was fine.

The doctor could see me right away. Shocking. She checked me over, did a urinalysis, blood work up, and chest/neck x-rays. A few days later, the results showed that everything was clear and normal except for a high white blood cell count. She thought I must be fighting something, but I showed no signs of infection – no cold, sore throat, sinus, bladder infection, lung or heart problem … nothing. Like I thought, I'm fine. This is just some strange growth that needs to be removed. I saw a guy once who had a lump that looked like a hard-boiled egg protruding from the side of his temple. Now that was a can't-help-but-gawk--turn-your-stomach--nasty-looking, gross lump, and he should have had that removed pronto! My lump wasn't even noticeable unless I pointed it out. Anyway, she referred me to a lymph specialist and suggested I go soon.

One week later, I was in the office of the lymph specialist. He reviewed the medical records I brought with me, then felt my neck, underarms, and abdomen.

He looked me in the eye and simply stated, "I can't be absolutely certain, but I think you probably have a lymphoma."

Huh?? I just looked at him, blinking, afraid to say anything, afraid I would lose control. My mind was blank. What does that mean? What's a lymphoma? I honestly didn't know, but it sure didn't sound like something I wanted. I had a sneaking suspicion, but I wanted him to tell me.

I asked, "What does that mean exactly?" I was trying to be brave, but my eyes were welling up. I was staring at the ceiling and blinking, but we both knew the tears were coming. He handed me a box of tissues and told me straight out, "Lymphoma is cancer in the lymph system."

CANCER. He said it. Oh my God. I might have cancer? How is that possible? Just the word CANCER makes me cry – and he's talking about ME having it, not some random person. What does this mean? Am I going to die? Be in pain? Shrivel up and be miserable? Lose all my hair? Be sick all the time? I have no idea what this means or what to expect. Horrible. Horrible. Horrible. Where did this come from?

I couldn't stop the tears. Poor fella – the worst part of his job must be telling patients that they have lymphoma. Talk about changing someone's life forever.

Pig Boy

In the fall of 1995, I got involved with someone who changed my life forever. Through my eyes, he was tall, dark, handsome, athletic, successful, a little arrogant, carefree and unruly, yet very sexy. I had to have him. He became the next love of my life ... or was he just an obsession? The first time I remember thinking "I want him" was an evening that we had just played beach volleyball and had gone to a friend's for a cookout and drinks afterwards. I don't remember his sportsmanship that night, but I do remember he had the audacity to pull up a chair in the kitchen and prop his dirty, sandy, sweaty feet on the end of the kitchen countertop! I couldn't believe his nerve and poor manners. Rude! Even more strange, I was not repulsed by his behavior, I was intrigued by it. What kind of person would do that? He didn't help with the cookout, just sat back, drank a beer, chatted, laughed and enjoyed himself. I felt compelled to find out what he was all about.

As luck would have it, the following week we attended a farewell party for a mutual friend. He came to the party with two gals he worked with, but I didn't think anything of it. Throughout the evening, we drank, we ate, we danced, we laughed ... had a super fun time, and he went home with me. I proceeded to find out what he was all about! He was all that and then some!! I was in love.

The next night, we went out with another group of friends – he met my sister and I met his brother. Again, we enjoyed an evening of drinking, eating, dancing, and laughing. At the end of the night, we drove my sister to her apartment. As she stepped out of the car and moved to close the door, the nail on her middle finger caught on his door's edge and painfully snapped, breaking deep into her nailbed. She screamed in pain and held her hand tight, the pain heating up and making her finger throb for hours and hours. To this very day, that fingernail consistently breaks. And believe me, every time it does, a few choice words are said in honor of the man behind the wheel, who eventually became known to us as Pig Boy. I felt terrible about Stephanie's fingernail, but I was excited to get home! From that point on, he and I saw each other almost every day for a week. We couldn't get enough of each other!

Chapter 10

"May you know the calming strength of
His hand upon you today.
Praying You'll Be Well Soon"
Card from the Thursday Morning Bible Study

Shortly after we all adjusted to my devastating news, Stephanie and I took off for Chicago. Thankfully, our routine is that she always drives back to the city – I can relax. I was emotionally exhausted and so relieved that now my family knows what's going on ... although now more people are going to find out about it. I don't like being the topic of discussion. I don't enjoy being the focus of anyone's pity. I don't want sympathy. I don't handle compassion well – I simply dissolve into tears. I do, however, believe in the power of prayer, positive thoughts and energy focused on healing. So, the more positive thoughts, the better. I believe I will be cured.

This Wednesday, the 2nd of November, I am scheduled for chemotherapy treatment #1. I'm curious to find out how this works. How do they do it? How will it make me feel? How long does it take? Will it make me sick? Will I be hungry? Will I lose my appetite and maybe some thigh cheese? Will I be able to keep working? How soon will my hair start falling out? How are the drugs going to affect me? So many questions, so many unknowns. I'm excited for my appointment because the sooner we get started, the sooner it will end. I don't know what to expect, but I'm ready to find out.

They told me to eat before every treatment, so I had a quick lunch and drove to the hospital. I know where the parking garage is now and had no trouble getting there on time. My first trip to the cancer center was spent driving around looking for the address, turning around after I passed it, feeling annoyed, frustrated, stressed and rushed! Cripes!!

Being directionally challenged is NO fun, and I seem to be hopeless. I just don't get it.

Stephanie took off from work again and met me in the reception area on the 21st floor of this amazing hospital. Per her instructions, I am to be careful what I touch, as she is. After all, hospitals are full of sick people! Open the doors with your gloves on or use your sleeve as a mitten – catch it with your foot if you can - punch the elevator button with your elbow, wash your hands when you get to the cancer center. We don't want other people's germs! I have a stash of hand sanitizer in my purse, in my car, on my desk at work … don't want to catch a cold or the flu or anything else. If I sneeze … sanitize. Blow my nose … sanitize. Someone else sneezes or coughs around me … hold my breath. Good grief … !!

Arriving at the cancer center, I checked in and picked up a buzzer. "When they are ready to draw your blood, we'll buzz you." One time years ago, our family went out to dinner at a steakhouse. After we put our name on the list with the hostess, we were asked to wait in the lobby until they called us. As we were milling about, the hostess called out a name. Before the words were even out of her mouth, that entire family literally sprang from their chairs and leaped up to the counter! Startled by their intense response, we all looked at each other and started giggling – we got such a kick out of it. We laughed and laughed … to this day, Stephanie and I giggle when we get called for a reservation. And I have to smile when my buzzer goes off.

I know everyone here either has a form of cancer or is here to support someone who has cancer. How depressing. Fortunately, the waiting room is not gloomy or dismal, but clean, bright, comfortable and almost cheerful. You can see the city and the lake from the windows. I would give my right arm to live in a place with this view! People are talking, reading, snoozing, or staring out the windows lost in thought while they wait. I'm kind of nervous, but I'm ready to get started. I will not cry. I am strong. I am here to be cured. This is just an experience I'm having to see what other people endure. Piece of cake. My lap buzzes and I spring out of my chair … ha! I'm the only one who thinks that's funny. Alas, they are ready for me. Oh boy – reality.

First stop is to get my blood drawn. What is my name? What are the last four digits of my social security number? Who is my doctor? She takes my hand, swabs a finger with alcohol, squeezes my finger pretty hard, which was cool because then I barely felt the little prick (reminds me of a couple of stories I won't be sharing – hee!) and collects my blood in a tiny vial for testing. Band-aid on and we're done. Fast and efficient – she needs to give a lesson to the folks at the blood center where I used to give blood several times a year. I've been told my days of giving blood are over. Good thing I gave while I could.

Back to the waiting room with another buzzer while they process my blood. Stephanie brought the gossip magazines so we have plenty to look at while we're waiting. Hollywood sure has a lot of couples cheating on each other. At least I'm not a celebrity, so every failed relationship I have isn't in the news! However, life and love with Pig Boy sure took a quick turn, and everyone in our lives knew about it.

Silent Treatment

After spending nearly every day together for a week, Pig Boy suddenly started canceling plans with me. No reason, no explanation – no communication. I saw him one morning in what looked to be a fairly intimate conversation with a brunette ... one of the gals he took to the farewell party the night we hooked up, as a matter of fact. Hm. And shortly after that, a very reliable source told me that he was dating a blonde. Is that right? Well, that would certainly explain all the secretive pages he would get when we were out! That was back in the days before cell phones. But seriously, would you return a page to another woman while you're on a date? Unless you're a doctor on call, I don't recommend it! He did it anyway – apparently, it was none of my business. Evil! I absolutely boiled inside, but at that time, I was trying to win him over, so I pretended it didn't bother me in the least. I was Miss Cool. Yet, the light was getting brighter ... I thought -- this guy is cheating on these <u>two</u> women with me. What an ass. And what does that make me??! Gosh.

What is wrong with this picture?? The Kelly of today would have paid attention to the red flags and ran far, far away super fast ... the Kelly of 10 years ago pretended it wasn't happening so she could get what she thought she wanted. At first, that is. I wanted him, and he was going to be with no one else but me and be happy about it. In the beginning, I did not pitch a fit nor get in his face until I got my way. As time passed, when I got mad, I yelled and screamed my accusations. His solution was to give me the silent treatment.

After a week of silent treatment and doing whatever he pleased with whomever he wished, he would come to me with as much of an apology as he could muster. Ha! He confessed that I was right, and I deserved an apology. I was winning! As his reward, I invited him on a trip to Mexico over Thanksgiving week with my family and about 12 of my girlfriends (much to their genuine dismay!). As my reward, he was honest with me about a "special friendship" with the brunette, the end of his relationship with the blonde, plus he gave me six red roses in a show of devotion to me. Naturally, I fell for it. We all went to Mexico for a week and had a mostly wonderful time. He and I then shared Christmas and rang in 1996 together. I just knew it was going to be the best year ever!

Chapter 11

"On my mind and in my heart.
We're thinking of you."

Card from Stephanie's good friend Amy

Stephanie and I are escorted back to the treatment room. It is a private, little hospital room complete with a bed, chair and footstool, computer, TV/DVD, and a sink. I settle onto the bed while Stephanie takes the chair. My Nurse Clinician came in to walk us through each drug again, its effect on the body, and to answer any questions we might have. I'm good; I'm brave; I'm not crying; I'm ready to go. Let's see what happens.

She started by giving me two Tylenol to swallow then inserting an IV in the top of my hand near my thumb, which I thought was unusual. Why not in the arm? I guess the hand works just as well, the vein was easy to find, it didn't hurt, and it must make it easier to push in the drugs. She pushed in two antinausea medications first, which pretty much relaxed me until my eyes glazed over. Stephanie said I looked and sounded drunk. She was glad to be there since there was no way I could drive home in that condition! It didn't hurt or feel any particular way at all. While I was feeling sleepy, I was trying to stay alert and chipper, to read a magazine and to carry on a conversation.

Next came the chemotherapy drugs:

1. Adriamycin
2. Bleomycin
3. Velban
4. Dacarbazine

The first two she pushed in with a syringe, and I could feel them going into my arm – cold, slightly uncomfortable, but not horrible by any stretch. The last two are drips – the final one takes an hour. The nurse reminded me that I may experience headache, constipation, or heartburn. It is okay to take over the counter medications, such as Tylenol, laxatives/stool softeners, and tums.

As soon as this treatment is over, I am supposed to go fill my prescriptions:

- Anzemet and Ativan for nausea
- Senna-S for constipation
- Bactrim-DS, which I think is an antibiotic/immune system booster
- Diflucan, which prevents mouth sores

I should also think about buying a thermometer, Tylenol, mouthwash, hand sanitizer, scar gel (for my neck) and some food I love to eat plus some juice. So much joy! It is expensive to be sick – I was shocked. I'm so thankful I have a good insurance plan.

The Nurse also warned me to call or page her if:

- I have a fever of 101 degrees or higher; if 102 degrees or higher, do not take any medication and call the emergency room right away
- I have uncontrolled nausea/vomiting/diarrhea
- I have pain or burning with urination
- I develop sores in my mouth
- I have any other questions or concerns

OK. I'm not sure if any of these things are going to happen to me. All I can say is that I am not looking forward to finding out, but here I am … treatments have started and now we'll see what happens.

She gave me more information and instructions:

1. Fevers are the most serious – as that could mean an infection or a problem of some kind – pay attention.

2. Mouth sores are caused by herpes – thankfully, I do not have this problem, so I hope not to experience this.

3. Eat light tonight and drink plenty of water and/or juice.

4. Don't take a daily vitamin the day before, the day of, or the day after treatment.

How am I supposed to remember all of this? I'm struggling just to stay awake. Stephanie is taking notes for me. Goody. I don't have to remember anything, as I can read, which is a blessing because I sure can't think right now.

After the last drop dripped, I was free to go. First, I had to literally run to the bathroom. Two hours of fluids being pumped into my body, and I could barely make it around the corner! My urine was a little pinkish and my mouth had a funny taste, but I wasn't drowsy or nauseous. Hooray! We walked to the drug store and bought everything I needed or might need. I was definitely ready to get home and relax, but I felt just fine. Stephanie agreed that I appeared to be fine. I drove home and ran to the bathroom again. Hope I don't end up with a bladder problem.

After being home for several hours, my doctor called to ask how I was feeling. I was certainly surprised and amazed by that! I was experiencing nothing – no nausea, no fever, no dizziness, no exhaustion – I felt normal. My nose was a little runny, and I had to pee frequently but that was it. I went to bed early because I could and thought I should but woke up every two hours during the night to pee. I had slight stomach cramps but they didn't amount to anything. I woke up in the morning feeling fine – hungry, not tired, no fever, no nausea – normal. WOW. I am so lucky. Speaking of lucky, my cousin Terry and his wife Shelli had a healthy baby girl named Keara yesterday, November 2, 2005. I will always remember her birthday!

Special Brunette #2

And back in 1996, I was feeling pretty lucky too. My boyfriend and I were getting along famously with only a fight here and there about the other "special brunette friend" in his life – their relationship was a real mystery to me, and I didn't like it or her one bit. Magically, she was fired (I had nothing to do with it!) so he wouldn't be seeing her every day anymore. What a shame. We (I mean "I") celebrated with a Valentine's weekend trip to Disney World! Sometime later, I saw a stack of photographs from one of his prior trips to Disney World with a former girlfriend – we went to the same places and even took the same pictures. So unoriginal and kinda creepy. The boy was a repeat offender in so many ways … this soon became very apparent.

Over the next few months, we had numerous discussions, turned into arguments, ending in silent treatment over this Special Brunette. She just would NOT go away. In the spring, he decided to move into a condo downtown, which I thought would be great as he would live closer to me! In fact, we flew to San Francisco to celebrate. We went here and there and all around … the whole time I'm getting flashbacks of this exact trip, as he had already gone to these exact places with Miss Disney World Former Girlfriend – because I had seen those pictures, too. Of course I brought it up on our last night and he flipped! He stomped out of the restaurant in silence (good thing he's not a screamer I guess) and left me to find my own way back. I had to laugh – it was just too damn funny. He was SO predictable. And I continued to love him anyway -- why?!

And guess what happened after he moved into his condo in the city? Unbeknownst to me, his mother immediately introduced him to a neighbor, who promptly and secretly became Special Brunette #2. We had the misfortune of "meeting" one day in the elevator on the way up to his condo. She had two snarling, fat, nasty, slobbering dogs chained to her wrists – her only redeeming quality it turns out. The first words out of her mouth were, "So this is

Kelly?" Huh-what? I was taken by surprise, as I had no idea who she was. I looked at him and he looked at me with eyes as wide as saucers, blinking. Clearly, he was busted. He gave ever so brief introductions while I stood in stunned silence and then he swooped me out the door onto his floor.

As soon as we stepped into his apartment, I hissed in an icy tone, "Care to explain that?" My eyes were daggers.

"Nothing to explain – she's a neighbor." Brother! I may have been born in the dark, but it wasn't yesterday. I glared, hands on hips, foot impatiently tapping, waiting for an explanation while I fantasized about lunging at him with a sword. Steam was shooting out of my ears as my blood started to boil, but his lips were sealed. He would say no more and imposed the predictable silent treatment. Slamming the door shut behind me, I stomped out in a foul and furious mood! He's impossible!! This guy was a liar, a cheater, and could not be trusted. How many examples does a girl need?!

No wonder he thought he could get away with it – who else would continue dating someone knowing this behavior was standard? He was evil, and I was torturing myself by staying with him. For some reason, I could not, would not completely let him go. And he would not stay away from me no matter how many times we broke up. I wanted to be so special to him that he would become honest and true and want only me! Surely he was worth the effort, so I forgave him after every apology extended with candy, flowers, and a sincere promise to turn over a new leaf. This man had more leaves than a forest, yet I always chose to believe him. Oink, oink, oink ... I should have known better.

Chapter 12

*"During your recovery, please take time to remember
what a courageous individual you are."*
Card handwritten by Sally

Life was sailing along smoothly with no changes to speak of other than
the lump in my neck, which was definitely getting smaller. That's good
news … I must be responding well to the drugs! Since I didn't feel
nauseous, tired or any different, I went about my business as usual
– dinner with friends, lunch dates with guys from random online
dating services (gotta keep trying, right?!), nights out with the girls,
crocheting baby afghans for all my pregnant girlfriends, organizing
closets, shopping, going to movies, and working out at the gym. A
little chemo isn't going to slow me down!

The weekend after my first treatment, my mom came up to Chicago
and went shopping with Stephanie and me for WIGS! Aahhh! I didn't
know if I was even going to lose my hair, but decided to be prepared just
in case. Besides, the doctor gave me a prescription for a hair prosthesis,
so my insurance had it covered. We went to a costume shop that was
actually highly recommended by the hospital for excellent wig choices.
I saw wigs of every length, color, and style. I didn't think that going
with bright blue, hot pink or neon orange would be wise. And we
were all determined to remain cheerful and positive to make it a fun
experience, even though the whole reason we were there was dismal
and depressing. We selected wigs in brown, auburn, blonde … in
very short, sort of short, shoulder length and long. Being a brunette,
I always wondered what it would be like to have long, gorgeous, silky
blonde hair. I flipped on some gorgeous, silky, blonde hair and turned
to face the mirror. Aahhh!!! HORRIBLE! HORRIBLE! No other
word for it than HORRIBLE! Seriously, I looked like death … pale,
drawn, vacant … even the store manager said from across the room

– "I wouldn't choose that one if I were you." HaHaHa! We had to laugh. Well, that problem was solved. I'll never be a blonde and now I know that I was never meant to be. They don't have more fun than this brunette anyway!

As it turns out, our favorite wigs were a short auburn and a flip-at-the-top-of-the-shoulder slightly less auburn but not quite brown one – both with bangs. I haven't had bangs since my former boss convinced me to grow them out and grow my hair longer in 2000 since that was all the rage then. Interestingly, these brought out the color in my face and made me look younger. Amazing! How fun is that?! What turned out NOT to be fun was that the $300 I spent on them was never reimbursed by my insurance company. Poo-Poo … apparently that was an exclusion in the small print I managed to skip over. Oh well, it is what it is.

Liar Liar

Pig Boy turned out NOT to be so fun either. We had one fight after another as I caught him in one lie after another. I'll never forget what his mother said to me one day … "He lies to you because of your reaction to the truth." Excuse me? Somehow it is MY fault that your son is a liar? Please.

He was a real peach through all of 1997. He took me to Italy for The Carnivale celebration in February. Shortly after we returned to Chicago, I learned that he flew off to Los Angeles with the snarly dog neighbor, Special Brunette #2 for a few days of Disneyland fun. You have GOT to be kidding me … FIGHT! I got apologies, flowers, and the new leaf speech again – this time in writing because I gave HIM the silent treatment. He must really be amused by these games. Who was the idiot here? What was wrong with me that I would excuse this behavior over and over? Was he really all that? Come on now.

Next he gave me a trip to Las Vegas for my summer birthday. Meanwhile, I noticed strange things scattered about: a random earring on his living room floor; women's sunglasses on the kitchen counter; snarly dog hairs in his car. FIGHT! We flew off to Vegas separately and never ran into each other until the flight home. I was still LIVID – he made me so mad. As usual, he played all the right cards for the next several weeks to win my forgiveness and then told me he was going to Italy by himself to visit family again in the fall. Hm ... sure.

While in Italy, he called me twice to say how much he missed me, loved me and couldn't wait to see me. I had sneaking suspicions and bad vibes about this trip though ... something didn't feel right. So, at the last minute, I made a mad dash to the airport to welcome him home. Fortunately, two of my girlfriends trailed me to the airport and held me back when he walked through the gate with – guess who? – snarly dog neighbor, Special Brunette #2. Inconceivable!! I would have beaten him into a grease spot had I been able to reach him. I was beside myself with anger and humiliation – I was beyond furious! I refused to speak to him – his old tactics of apologies, flowers, and phone calls would never work again.

He absolutely could not stand knowing that I thought he was evil and mean, and he went out of his way to reach out to me in friendship. By Christmas and with the gift of diamond earrings that I had wanted for years, I forgave him yet again. And the idiot would still be who? We spent New Year's together, but it wasn't magical or even fun, as I truly didn't trust him and could not believe one word he said. Over the next month, he made it too easy to catch him in more lies. Finally, all the deceit pushed me over the edge, and I had all I could take in one lifetime. I detached myself from him emotionally. I no longer wanted him. His evilness killed my obsession and exhausted my supply of forgiveness. Enough time wasted, I was finally ready to move on with my life without him in it.

I ran into him this summer still playing beach volleyball with the same team he did back then. He is married and has two children – shocking! He actually stopped by my office one day shortly after that so I could meet his little darlings – a boy and a girl. They were cute and sweet, very hard to believe they were his offspring. We had an awkward visit, but it was refreshing to realize it didn't matter what he said because he's not my problem.

What's funny is that every now and then he runs into my sister, who still hates him with a vengeance because of all the heartache he caused me, not to mention the injured fingernail still causing her grief! He knows this and cowers at the sight of her because he is afraid of what insult she might fling at him in the presence of one of his colleagues. She and I delight in the power of possibility!

Chapter 13

*"What a bummer! You're now a member of the
'Chemo Club' – Yuk!"*

Card handwritten by Aunt Linda

Life continued to sail along smoothly. I went to the gym two or three nights a week, went out for dinner with friends, went to movies … nothing was different. Could I be any luckier? This was certainly not what I assumed life would be like while undergoing cancer treatment. I felt good, I had energy, and I worked like crazy.

However, one thing I did notice was my hair falling out by the handful … it was actually happening. Each morning, I vacuumed my pillow and the bathroom floor; I was very careful not to let too much go down the bathtub drain. I've always had thick hair and lost a good amount of it every day anyway, but this was something else! In spite of the amount I lost, I really couldn't tell the difference – nobody could tell – it looked the same. Interesting … wonder how this will progress.

On November 15, 2005, just one day before my second chemo treatment, I worked all day as usual but had the chills. I just could NOT get warm. I wore my coat, bought a heating pad and sat on it, held it, put it on my lap but nothing warmed me up. Go home? Heavens no … too much to do! After work, I was simply miserable and walked to the gym in tears of misery and frustration. I cancelled the session with my trainer, then sat in the steam room believing that would surely warm me up. I was boiling when I came out, then took a shower and was cold again. Oh no, something must be wrong. Yipes! Is this what happens?! I have no idea, but I'm not enjoying it.

I went home and took my temperature. I had a fever of 101.4 and probably had it all day but that hadn't occurred to me or anyone else. My instructions say, "If you get a fever of 101 or more, call the emergency room." I paged my nurse practitioner, who called me back and said to go to the emergency room. She would call ahead, and they would be expecting me. Feeling miserable, scared, and cold, I called Stephanie and through my sobs asked her to come get me. I laid in bed with my coat, hat and mittens on until she picked me up. I shuffled out to the car and shivered the 15 minutes it took to get to the hospital all the while trying not to cry. I hate being sick and needing help. Hate it! So this is what happens … the disease and side effects of treatments were kicking in … this is going to be horrible. How do children and old people handle this? Seriously.

I've been to an emergency room maybe four times in my life. As a child, so I'm told, I was standing on the seat in a pickup and fell out the door when my uncle turned the corner – got stitches. (Brilliant!) Once when I was in 5th grade (not at band camp but at the movie with friends), I found a tick in my hair, freaked out, and insisted on going to the emergency room. My dad is a veterinarian – turns out he could have taken it out for free, as dogs get them all the time. (Dumb – never entered my mind.) When I was a freshman in high school, Stephanie and I were trying out a t-bar at the ski slopes. We had just been instructed NOT to sit on it, so when the bar came up behind us and tapped the back of our knees, naturally we sat down. The bar collapsed and wham – I got hit in the mouth with it. Ended up in the ER to get stitches. (Still have a scar from that one.) In the mid-90s, Stephanie was walking her bicycle down some stairs and the pedal spikes literally gouged out the back of her calf – aaahhh! Still turns my stomach just thinking about it. The next morning when she couldn't walk, I took her to the ER. The doctor must have given her 20 shots to numb her calf (Thank God!) and proceeded to dig, scrape, scrub and clean that wound. I was horrified watching, but she didn't flinch even once and felt nothing at the time. If she had felt anything for even a moment, I would have had to leave the room. Horrible! Believe me, she still has the scar.

When I arrived in the ER around 8:30 pm, I checked in, and indeed, they were expecting me. A nurse met me right away, gave me a face mask (to protect me from all the sickness lurking in the waiting room), took my temperature and blood pressure. I looked and felt awful, but there were some equally as pitiful patients waiting for help. Stephanie and I were ushered into the waiting room where we sat and waited and waited. Finally, a nurse took us to a separate room to wait when she realized I was at a stage in my disease where my white blood cell levels were so low that the possibility for infection was very high. I laid on the couch in a little room and dozed while Stephanie sat and waited and waited. At 12:30 a.m. they admitted me to the hospital for blood tests to find out what caused the fever. They gave me Tylenol, which quickly made me feel better, and I could not stay awake. Stephanie would be talking to me, and I would find myself waking up – oops, fell asleep again. She decided to go home, as I was obviously going to sleep fine. I was to call her in the morning with my test results.

A team of doctors came to see me in the morning. My test results showed nothing – no infection, nothing unusual … nothing at all. Hm. My temperature was down to 99 degrees, I felt fine, but they were keeping me for observation. Friends visited me during lunch hour, brought magazines, puzzles, chocolate (!), smiles and stories. I read, napped and watched daytime TV … worthless programming. By mid-afternoon, my temperature was normal and I napped a little more. What a great day! Somebody brought me breakfast (unfortunately, my scrambled eggs were covered with green peppers – foul – can't eat that!) and lunch, so I had nothing to do but relax – I didn't feel sick, I wasn't cold, I wasn't even bored. Since my test results were negative and my primary doctor was out of town, they decided to keep me overnight again.

By 9:30 pm, I had a headache, chills and a temperature that spiked to 101.7. What's going on?! I hadn't left the room, was on a constant IV drip, and had so much fluid that I had to run to the bathroom every hour. The nurse took more vials of blood. Something must be wrong, and they would not release me until I was there for 24 hours with no fever. Again, they gave me Tylenol. I finally warmed up and fell asleep. I didn't have any other symptoms, so it was a mystery what was causing the fevers. I woke up numerous times during the night, as the nurses would not leave my door closed. Is that too much to ask for crying out loud?! GOSH. Too much light and too much racket makes me cranky! I'm sure every nurse got "the look" for disturbing me, and I know I was far from pleasant. I did, however, become highly skilled at maneuvering my IV into the bathroom, which was a good thing since I barely allowed enough time to get in there. The nurse asked me to pee in a measuring bowl to see if I had enough output. Ha! After calling her in twice to empty it, she realized my system was working just dandy.

Day 2 in the hospital was more of the same. No green peppers in my eggs today – that was good news. Other good news: no pain, diarrhea, constipation, fever, infection … I've got nothing. Lungs are clear and heart is strong. I read all my magazines, ate all my chocolate, napped, made phone calls and the nurse put my arm in a bag so I could shower. I look hideous – no makeup, flat hair and a lovely green hospital gown. The doctors visited, had nothing to report, and my fever did not return. If I'm still without a fever in the morning, I can go home. I'm not really worried, as I don't feel bad. I'm well rested and well fed. I can almost be cheerful.

I'd hate to be a nurse – patients can be gross, nasty, and miserable people. Actually, my first year of college was nursing school, but I couldn't handle the labs. Even the simplest tasks like taking blood pressure or pricking a finger … ahh! Inflicting pain on another person made my stomach turn – just couldn't do it. Could you imagine changing the gauze on bed sores and tracheotomies? No way. I don't regret my choice to switch career paths to office administration, but at my advanced age today, I believe I could be a nurse after all. In fact, I believe I would get a charge out of inflicting pain on a person or two … or three!

Day 3 … they released me to go home because my friend Becky is staying with me for the weekend, and I won't be alone. Besides, all tests revealed zilch – nothing caused my fever, it is just part of my disease. So, onward and forward into treatment #2 next week. On my way home, I stopped by the drug store to pick up a few things and stopped at my friend Anne's to pick up some delicious food that she made for me. I cancelled dinner plans and a night out with friends this week. Boo! That does not make me happy, but better safe than sorry at this point.

Once I got home, I started to feel congested. I called my nurse practitioner who told me to take some Theraflu, go to bed, and call her in the morning. Not much of a fun visit for Becky! On Saturday, we are supposed to get together with my friends and their kids, then go to the Lighting of Michigan Avenue, which has become an annual tradition for my sister and me. No go. I have to cancel everything as I must have a cold – I feel awful and just want to stay in bed. Is this what happens after one lousy treatment?! If that's the case, this is going to be a long and dreadful winter. However, on Sunday, I felt better. After Becky left, I went to visit friends for the afternoon. A common cold is not going to keep me at home and in bed all day!

By Sunday night, my chest was feeling very congested and heavy but I managed to sleep. I went to work on Monday morning as usual, and by noon, I absolutely could not breathe. Every word required a huge breath to go on to my next word. Have you ever felt suffocated? Way back in the days before I could swim, I used to play in the kiddie pool. One day while I was crawling under 8" of water, some vicious child sat on me! I remember the heavy weight on my back, the inability to take a breath, not being able to move ... what must have been a few seconds felt like an eternity and the end of my life. My struggle finally freed me, and I was able to catch my breath! I'll never ever forget that feeling. And there I was sitting at my desk in my office feeling like I was under water with a huge weight holding me down – I could not breathe. Was I going to have a heart attack? Was I going to suffocate? As I started to panic, my work partner and very good friend, Rod, rushed me to the emergency room and checked me in. I paged my nurse practitioner on the way over, barely able to speak through my sobs and lack of air. Cold, weak, scared and uncertain about what would happen next, I was ushered into a private room the moment I arrived.

The ER doctor gave me an asthma treatment and all the pressure was released – I could breathe again. After 20 minutes, the pressure was back, and I couldn't breathe. The ER doctor gave me another treatment and suddenly I turned red and swollen with hives. I threw off the blanket and wanted to rip my clothes off as I became an itching, scratching fool! What the hell?! In rushed the nurse to give me a

Benadryl shot to stop the itching which practically knocked me into a coma. Almost instantly, I was like a dried up noodle licking dry lips with a cotton tongue. As horrible as that made me feel, at least I could breathe, so they left me alone on the cold, hard table and peered at me around the curtain every so often. Shortly thereafter, my breathing became labored again but they couldn't give me another treatment since they knew I would most likely have another itchy-scratchy reaction. Now what?! I'm not a sick person, why is this happening?? The doctor prescribed a nose spray and sent me home to get some rest. How is that going to be possible?!

I spent the evening coughing, blowing my nose, and trying to catch my breath. My heart was pounding, and I could not breathe! What good would it do to go to the emergency room again? I tried lying down, sitting up, showering ... nothing made me feel better or helped me to breathe and I was simply exhausted. Should I call a cab? What is the ER going to do for me? Sometimes when you have a cold and your chest is congested, if you can just take in enough air, a good breath breaks through. No such luck.

More coughing, more blowing ... I needed to calm down. If I just lie very, very still under piles of heavy, warm blankets with my body curled around my heating pad and take very, very slow deep breaths, I can work through it. I'm still cold, miserable, tired, and afraid each breath is going to be my last. I can't get warm. I must have a fever. I can't breathe. I can't take this all night. What am I going to do? Be calm, breathe in, breathe out, stay calm, breathe slowly ... I had to talk myself through it for what felt like hours. Breathe, stay calm, breathe, stay warm ... I can do it. I fell asleep.

Miraculously, I lived through the night. All of my tissues were gone and I was still congested, but I was alive and breathing in spite of my cardboard, mucus coated thick tongue. Gross! Will I ever feel normal again? I despise being sick. Regardless, gotta get up and go to work. However, by mid-afternoon, I was exhausted and ready to go home to get some sleep. Tomorrow is treatment #2 after all, and I want it so I can get on with the program. Off to bed ... I can't wait to crawl into the warmth and sleep the day away.

Chapter 14

"Wouldn't it be nice if our lives were like VCRs...
... and we could "fast forward" through the crummy times?"
Card from Erika

Being Thanksgiving week, I have a lot to be thankful for in the grand scheme of things. The cancer was discovered early enough to be treated, I'm otherwise healthy and young enough to handle the treatment, and I have very caring family and friends to help me through the process. I need emotional support more than anything else – not pity mind you, but the support of friends to keep me active and involved in life. While my hair continues to fall out, I try to stay brave by realizing it's only hair ... it will grow back. But being a Leo, hair is important! Full, thick hair is a sign of health and vitality, and I have always had it and have always loved it. I can't stand sweeping it up off the floor every day – it just breaks my heart and makes me sad. All I can do is wipe up my tears along with locks of hair. My heart just aches, and I feel so alone, ugly and depressed. How do I handle this? What am I supposed to do? I'll need to get a grip, that's what. I will not allow this to change who I am.

Stephanie is meeting me at the hospital today for Treatment #2. Assuming that goes well, I am inviting two girlfriends from work over for dinner and to shave my head. Might as well get it over with now and stop fretting about how much I'm losing every day. I've got four wigs, so I might as well use them!

Stephanie was waiting for me at the hospital. They drew my blood and called us back for the treatment. My white blood cell count went from 17.7 at my first treatment to 7.1 – the drugs are working. The lump on my neck has nearly disappeared – more proof the drugs are working. All good news! I was also looking forward to losing a few pounds, which is one of the possible side effects to receiving chemotherapy. The nurse took my vitals -- blood pressure is normal, temperature is normal, weight is higher. What?! Not only have I not lost my appetite, I'm eating AND gaining weight. Fabulous. I'll be bald AND fat – this is great news.

The technician gave me the anti-nausea drugs and then the chemo. I didn't get as loopy this time and felt absolutely fine when the session was over. Clearly, I am handling the treatments and do not need help to get home, so Stephanie and I decided that I am on my own from this point forward. No need for her to take time off work to babysit me. In fact, the last drug is a one-hour IV drip that I can take a nap through. Works for me … love naps!

After I got home, super friends Erin and Debbie came over with some Thai food. Yum! Perhaps I should cut back and only eat half. No way, man … I gobbled the whole thing. Love that pad se ewe! Debbie brought a movie that we tried to watch, but I just couldn't concentrate. We laughed and talked -- anything to take my mind off what was coming next and to delay it as long as possible. (I was thinking: I'm not ready to shave my head yet, I'm just not. I still have hair after all.) Finally, we got down to business. They brushed and combed and the hair came out and out and out getting thinner and thinner, but I still seemed to have plenty. I got out the scissors, and Erin started chopping. Chop, chop, chop. Yipes! She's not a trained stylist, but actually, it didn't look too bad short, so we decided just to cut it really short instead of shaving it off. What a relief! My hair hasn't been this short since Kindergarten, yet I kinda like it. I can live with this. Debbie got out the vacuum and swooped it all up so I didn't have to see it. These gals are the BEST! I don't know what I would do without them. I'm so lucky.

Really Great Guy

Speaking of lucky, after I finally realized Pig Boy would never be trustworthy, I met an Irishman during another beach volleyball game. He was tall, cute, athletic and fun! We immediately starting hanging out and had a great summer ... running, playing volleyball, roller blading, attending street festivals, movies, dinners, Cubs games, concerts, and comedy clubs. Every day was something fun! Alas, he was a rebound fling and my heart wasn't in it, so I had to let him go when I met a Really Great Guy at a Cubs game in the fall.

Really Great Guy and I hit it off immediately! I was smitten and thought he was spectacular. He was the big, athletic type; had lots of good friends; was adventurous and loved to travel; owned his own business and worked hard; he was kind, thoughtful, fun, and introduced me to his family and included me in his life. This was just what I always wanted! Yet I was still carrying mental baggage from the last three years with an evil man I couldn't trust, and I found myself looking for flaws in this Really Great Guy. I made sure I found them, too – turned mole hills into mountains!

I had even gone so far as to institute a "6 Month Rule" so I would never waste years of my life with the wrong guy ever again. If I was not madly IN LOVE within six months, that was it – relationship over – hang it up – move on. Made perfect sense to me at the time. He had no idea, of course, because I didn't tell him about my rule. We had a mostly wonderful time together but after six months, he had not declared his love for me, so I broke up with him. He was surprised and confused and realized he did love me. By then I had already made up my mind that it was over, had detached myself from him emotionally, and had cut off any possibility of working things out. In a very cruel, horrible, rotten and mean way that I'm too embarrassed to repeat – I cut him out of my life. It was the most evil thing I've ever done, and I still regret it. Did I give myself cancer?!

For a long time I did feel terribly guilty about how I treated him, as I'm not a mean-spirited person, and he clearly did not deserve to be treated so badly. Chicago can be a small city, and I have run into him numerous times during the last several years. He was always gracious and friendly, yet anxious to go. I could certainly understand that! Last summer, however, we briefly reconnected. He had been dating a gal for four years and was planning their wedding when everything fell apart. He had been single for a year when we got together again. Things were awkward at first, but we still got along great and enjoyed each other's company. I thought we might actually have a second chance! What I learned was that he had finally reached the point in his life that had been his goal all those years ago and was preparing to move out of state. He gave me the gift of forgiveness before he left, and I'm very happy to say we are friends.

Chapter 15

"Just remember, you're an amazing person
and a true inspiration to me."

Note handwritten by Debbie Z.

When I bought my condo, our family started a tradition of having Thanksgiving dinner at my place. I make the turkey, potatoes, and stuffing while mom makes her famous cranberry salad (my favorite!) and pecan pie, and Stephanie makes the green bean casserole, veggie tray and shrimp cocktail. This year, Stephanie decided I didn't need the stress of hosting, so we packed our bags and went to the Kettles' for the holiday. Mom and Stephanie pretty much made everything while I did basically nothing but set the table. Even though I have cancer, I am still perfectly capable of cooking and helping out; however, I am certainly not opposed to acting like a male by sitting in the living room, sipping a drink, watching TV or reading, and waiting to be called into the dining room for dinner. What a life!

We ate a delicious meal and had no talk of cancer or the hospital stint I had recently endured. No reason to worry anyone, as I'm going to be fine. We are all aware that I am fighting this disease with harsh drugs, but I still have hair, energy, and my appetite. While I appear to be the same Kelly as always, I was being given special kid-glove treatment, so I spent the balance of my time at home sitting on the couch crocheting a blanket for my cousin's baby, listening to football, and napping. Nothing puts all of us to sleep after a big turkey dinner like a football game!

Dapper Dave

Of all the turkeys I've dated, I chuckle when I think about an older gentleman I spent some time with one summer. During an outdoor social event at one of Chicago's yacht clubs, I was getting great pleasure from a lovely, balmy evening with a few girlfriends milling about and enjoying drinks and music while checking out the scene. As we were discussing the current state of eligible men, I noticed two seasoned Dapper Daves sauntering towards us. The taller of the two (styling in white linen shirt and pants, navy blue blazer and leather boat shoes with no socks) walked right up to me, took my hand in his, looked directly into my eyes and asked in all seriousness, "Are you in love?"

With such a unique approach, I was taken by surprise and smiled. Instead of saying, "You goofball – get away from me," I said, "No, why do you ask?" I'm sure he had a clever response, but I don't recall. I do recall that he was by my side for the rest of the evening buying drinks for all of us gals and being as witty, charming and attentive as possible. He invited us to go yachting on his friend's boat and would not take no for an answer. Dapper Dave (DD) promised a fun afternoon cruising Lake Michigan on a gorgeous yacht. He would pick me up, and I could bring one of my girlfriends to keep his friend company. Sounded like great fun to me!

The following weekend, I invited my more-than-willing girlfriend, Colleen, to join us for an afternoon on the boat. We had a sunny, bright, perfect summer day – we couldn't be more excited! DD pulled up to the curb in an old, huge, bench seat Cadillac and insisted that we both sit in the front next to him. OK – whatever. We were then treated to an Elvis cassette tape while DD happily sang along. He had recorded only one Elvis song that played over and over and over. I looked at Colleen, and we rolled our eyes and chuckled – a small price to pay for a fun afternoon on a private yacht!

On round two of Elvis' song, we stopped at another apartment. Two scantily clad, tanned and gleeful girls came bouncing toward the car with their beach bags, big sunglasses and cell phones. As they hopped in the back seat, Colleen and I both turned to DD with a look of ... what on earth?! Who are these tramps? His friend had invited them and asked that he pick them up. Good grief. Oh well, we'd make the best of it. Shortly thereafter, we pulled over to pick up two more gals. "Goody," I smirked and blinked my eyes at DD, as if I had anything to say about whom they invited to their boat. What a lovely day this was turning out to be!

At last, we arrived at the harbor, poured out of the car, and schlepped all of our things and the gaggle of women to the boat. Magically, the "yacht" was already brimming with women of all ages and appearances. Imagine that! DD and his two male associates managed to get us all onto the boat with not an inch to spare. I'm not sure what qualifies a boat as a yacht, but we certainly had enough females on board to qualify as a sorority reunion. Fortunately, we didn't have to sing any songs, play any games, or scrub the deck. We claimed our seats and off we sailed!

Actually, I was relieved that we had extra passengers on board so that Colleen and I could relax and enjoy the sun and wind without entertaining DD. Much to my surprise, he was not interested in the hot young chicks but preferred to sit with us and exchange stories. As when we met, DD was attentive and made sure we always had a drink in hand while he himself drank only water. Turns out, he has led a colorful life – bodyguard to the *stars, world traveler, and entrepreneur. He was quite interesting, and I was intrigued to find out what he would tell us next. Before we knew it, we were back to the harbor and the cruise was over.*

Afterwards, DD and his friend escorted Colleen and me to dinner. We had a lovely evening with amusing conversation and live music. This launched a routine for DD and me. Once a week, he would pick me up in his Cadillac at 5:30 p.m. while Elvis sang his song. We were always the first ones seated at whichever restaurant he chose, and he always ordered a salad, soup (but only the broth, please), salmon, broccoli and fresh berries for dessert. He only drank water. I could have whatever I pleased. After dinner, he drove me home, walked me to the door, and left with a kiss on the cheek. He never asked if I wanted to do anything else, always had me home no later than 7:30 p.m., and never asked to come in nor invited me to his place. Was he married? Did he have another date? Was he always headed out to guard a super star? I never asked, and he never told. This arrangement was great ... far be it from me to upset the basket!

One evening as DD walked me to my door, I was completely surprised when he wrapped me in his arms and gave me an intense, deep, long kiss. WOW. I didn't know what to say. I was stunned and rooted to the sidewalk, merely blinking my eyes at him in shock. That was totally out of character! He sauntered away in silence with a big smile on his face. He must have a plan.

Sure enough, the next week, he invited me out to his home in the suburbs where I would have my own suite for the weekend to celebrate my birthday. He settled me into my room, then gave me a tour of the house and his worldly collections and photo walls, which were covered with the famous people he had guarded over the years. He was neat, clean, and I didn't see any signs that another woman was in his life. DD treated me to a shopping spree complete with clothes, shoes, perfume and dinner at his favorite local diner.

Back at the house, we settled into the couch and watched a movie, after which we got to know each other a little more personally. He was interesting, and I was beginning to trust him. Who would have thought?

Chapter 16

*"I've thought of you so much and wonder how you
are getting along...but know that you will come thru this."*
Note handwritten by Gram McPherron

The next few weeks were life is usual ... brunch, lunch, and dinner with friends, workouts at the gym, open houses for work, and crocheting baby afghans. So many babies due in the spring! I have also been enjoying holiday parties, shopping and decorating for Christmas. My friend Christine gave me a DVD player as an early Christmas gift so I could watch movies at home away from the germs of a theater. I really need to be careful not to catch anything – not a cold or the flu or anything that will prevent me from having a treatment. And right now, as my hair, eyebrows and eyelashes continue to fall out, I'm perfectly happy to spend time at home alone in my jammies and stocking hat.

By the end of treatment #4, I settled into a routine at the hospital of kicking off my shoes, sitting under a blanket, and then taking a nap while the last drug was administered through an IV. I never sleep in my wigs at home, but decided to try my nap while wearing one. It's like sleeping in a helmet – kind of awkward but sure didn't keep me awake! I get so tired. Much to my amazement, each treatment is as stress free as the last. They don't hurt, and they don't make me sick. I get to take a snooze, then go home for dinner, watch a movie, and go to bed early. This is certainly not what I expected, and I am so thankful.

Mom called to say she was worried about my health and thinks I don't always have to be so brave and do everything on my own. Actually, I'm not being brave – I'm just lucky that everything is going smoothly and easily so far.

Kelly Molchan

Las Vegas

After my weekend with DD in the suburbs, our easy breezy relationship mysteriously took a dive. He was suddenly traveling, working a lot, or simply not calling. Our pattern was broken, and I didn't hear from him nearly as much. Go figure. He called one day to say his aunt, who lived in Florida, was ill, and he was going to visit. In two weeks, he wanted us to take a little jaunt to Las Vegas for the weekend and have some fun. He asked if I would book the flights, the hotel, and buy the show tickets for us ... he would pay me back. Since I worked with a travel agency frequently for work, I was happy to do it and jumped all over it!

That Saturday, he called to say his aunt had passed and he would not be able to go to Vegas after all and would I cancel the trip. I told him I could cancel the show tickets and the hotel, but the flights would have to be used later with a change fee. I was disappointed, but totally understood, so I promptly cancelled the reservations.

Four days later, DD called to say he was home and did I want to spend the weekend with him in the suburbs. Excuse me?? This smelled very fishy, and I didn't like it one bit. Why did I have to cancel a trip we could have easily taken?

"I thought you were in Florida at a funeral – what are you doing home?"

"Oh, the funeral is over, and I'm back. Let's just spend the weekend here."

"What about the $1,200 plane tickets I just booked on my credit card that we could actually use since you're back?"

"No, let's just stay here." My blood started to boil.

"I don't understand this. No, I do not want to spend the weekend in the suburbs - absolutely not." I slammed the phone in his ear – if only I had a whistle, he'd be deaf!

My intuition kicked in, and I nearly flipped out of my chair. I knew something was going on that I didn't know about! My intuition is almost always right, and I didn't like the feel of this one toot. Evil!! He was NOT telling me the truth, and he was taking advantage of me. He was taking me for a fool, and I would not have it! I called the travel agency to find out how I could get my money back for those tickets. If I could produce a death certificate, they would refund my money. Oh please, there was no death in the family, I was certain of that. What a creep ... I could not believe it.

I called him to ask for a copy of the death certificate. "Ha!" he said. "I don't have a death certificate – get real." I was beside myself with anger ... I'm an idiot. What happened here? Who is this guy anyway? In fact, if this man comes anywhere near me, I would have to be restrained to keep from choking him to death. I was livid! (He must be the same breed as Pig Boy ... how do I get involved with these people?!) When I calmed down the following week, I called again to ask him to reimburse me for the flights we didn't take. He wasn't interested. Again, my blood boiled! Unbelievable.

I promptly called one of my lawyer friends, told him the story, and asked him to write a letter demanding payment for the flights, or we would take him to small claims court. Shortly after mailing that letter, I receive a curt reply stating that he owed me nothing and would see me in court. The nerve! Thinking he duped me, I never heard from him again. What an evil rat.

After discussing the situation with my lawyer friend, we determined that the time, stress and aggravation of taking him to court would cause me more grief than he was worth. The fabulous news is that my travel agent did refund my money! (Obviously, this occurred pre-911.) So poo-poo, the joke's on DD – what a loser.

I get great satisfaction out of knowing he must have felt guilty. In fact, a few years after the incident, I was in a restaurant when he walked through the door and made direct eye contact with me almost immediately. My initial reaction was to smile and wave, and as I was lifting my hand, I remembered what happened. I dropped my hand, turned my smile upside down into the meanest look I could muster, and prepared to march right over his face. He spun around, made a beeline out the door, and vanished into the dark. Run, DD, Run! Evil never triumphs!!

Chapter 17

"I wanted you to know you have people in places you may have since forgotten that care about you...I can and will be there for you."
Handwritten by friend Daniel T.

Christmas season arrived relatively stress free, as our family decided not to do a gift exchange this year. Instead, we kids are sending mom and dad on a cruise for their 50th wedding anniversary in March in lieu of a party. That's a gift that will extend for quite awhile! Meanwhile, I was enjoying a little shopping for friends, wrapping presents, dining with small groups of friends, and attending a few parties. In fact, I was feeling spunky for my office holiday party and wore a long, red wig with a white fur headband and a sassy outfit, even though the biggest snowstorm of the year hit that day and the roads were a mess. The guests at the party who didn't know me sure got a kick out of my outfit and looked at me like they wondered who on earth I thought I was in that get-up. Might as well have fun with it!

Much to my surprise, I still feel just fine and treatments continue to be smooth and painless. My hair falls out a little more each day, the eyebrows and eyelashes are dwindling, and I'm waiting for the other shoe to drop. My nurses tell me that if I am not getting sick from treatments now, I most likely won't. Wow! I can hardly believe it.

Regardless of my hairlessness, I have been on a few dates lately. When I decide they aren't "the one," I casually mention that I'm wearing a wig, as I'm going through cancer treatments. Without trying to appear shocked and horrified, they pay for our drinks and bolt out the door! Ha! I'm not trying to be mean, but a lot of people are so afraid of the unknown, their reactions just crack me up. Can you "catch" cancer by sitting next to someone who has it? Hardly, but you'd think so the way they react. I will never understand boys, men, whatever they call themselves. Yes, I want to be loved and to give love in return, but is it worth all the drama, the compromising, the consulting and careful words you have to use ... and men think women are fragile. Use one wrong word or phrase or heaven forbid have an expectation, and they freak out! You're asking too much – taking away their freedom – using them for entertainment. Good grief -- I don't need it!!

Introduce Indiana

However, a former boyfriend of mine reached out to me recently after mutual friends (who introduced us a couple years ago) told him what I was going through lately. He is handsome, sweet, thoughtful, kind, fun, generous, owns his own business, is a good athlete and a great dad to two grown boys – sounds ideal. Except, he lives in Indiana of all places. He and his boys are going to Mexico for Christmas, and he wants to get together for lunch when he gets back. Hmm ... why did we break up?

When we first met, I was visiting our mutual friends in Indiana. After dinner, they decided we should stop by his house so I could meet him and visit with him because he was going through a hard time and was feeling depressed. We drove out in the country for what seemed like miles, and I had no clue where we were. We turned off the main road onto a lane that became a one-car-width rocky path beside a small lake, which then went up a steep hill surrounded by woods. At the top of the hill stood a little A-frame house with a stone patio and a fabulous three-level wooden deck: one level with a big table, chairs and grill; the next level down was a hot tub big enough for plenty of friends; and more steps led down to a fire pit where you could sit near the flames and roast hot dogs and corn on the cob. How charming!

The house was dark and the only sign of possible life was an SUV with its doors wide open, and the overhead light was very dim as if the battery was just about to die. How long had the doors been open? Was he inside? Did he hurt himself? Yipes... it was dark and spooky, and I whispered, "I don't like this ... we'd better go!"

Instead, we decided to poke our heads around – nobody was in the truck (I could only imagine what we could have discovered!), nobody was on the ground beside the truck, nobody appeared to be in the house. Was he ok? Where was he? He didn't answer their phone calls.

We stood there contemplating what to do next when suddenly another SUV tore up the lane, rounded the corner and screeched to a halt in a cloud of dust. The doors flew open as if the vehicle's seats were on fire, and two men leaped out – apparently, Indiana and one of his sons had arrived. When the dust settled, I saw the white flash of two gorgeous smiles. Yeowza ... father and son were hotties! I perked up and thought perhaps we should stick around. After greetings and introductions were made, Indiana explained that the doors to the SUV were standing open because it had rained in and the seats were wet – they were just drying it out while they were at a movie. That was a huge relief!

Turns out Indiana had built the marvelous deck himself, and he invited us to jump in the hot tub and enjoy a cool beverage. Works for me! We put on bathing suits, slipped into the steamy water, and listened as he told his story. I'm pretty sure I was nodding as if paying attention, but I was mostly noticing his strong arms and broad shoulders, his handsome face with the sexy smile, and wondering why on earth any woman would leave this man. He was clearly distraught and confused by her absence and had asked her repeatedly to come home. He was trying to convince himself he was ready to accept the loss and move on with his life. I was certainly willing to help him! In my opinion, she was a fool, and I saw this beautiful jewel of a man just waiting to shine.

I did my best to polish that jewel and make it mine, but I have zero tolerance for being chosen by default. Long story short, Indiana needed more time to sort out his life. I know he saw good things in me and potential with us, but he wasn't ready and by golly my clock was ticking ... I wanted somebody who was emotionally available in the present. And now here it is nearly two years later, Indiana is divorced and I'm still unattached. Go figure. I wonder if he has a girlfriend now...I'm afraid to ask. Guess I'll find out during lunch in a few weeks.

Introduce Arizona

At my advanced age, Indiana was not the first man I dated with a newly broken marriage. A grade school crush I had stayed in touch with since fifth grade started visiting me in Chicago a few years ago, as he had business in the suburbs regularly, even though he lived in Arizona. He was always a big flirt, which was fun but harmless, because he was married. I wouldn't cross that line and he knew it – although he gave it his best shot over the years. I invited him to a Christmas party that year at my apartment and found out he had just gotten a divorce. He was free, but I was seeing someone at the time who I wasn't really crazy about, but he was at the party. Arizona and I had an undeniable "thing" that I suspected we would eventually explore.

By the end of January, Arizona had convinced me to fly out for a visit. He said he had a big, beautiful home where I would have my own room, and he would be a complete gentleman. Does this sound like Dapper Dave or what?! The red flag should have gone up, but I was too excited to get to a warm climate for a few days, and we had agreed to drive out to San Diego to visit my grandma, aunt, uncle and cousins. He has known my grandma as long as he has known me, so they would not be strangers. Little did I know at the time that she was not a big fan of his!

He called regularly, sent roses for Valentine's Day, and arranged for my flights (with his frequent flyer miles, I'm pretty sure!). When I arrived, he picked me up at the airport, and we immediately had dinner with his parents to get reacquainted. We had a lovely evening, and I only felt a slight twinge when he and his mother went out for a smoke. Aah! Smoking is a HUGE pet peeve of mine, and he knew it. He promised to quit and would do so when he was ready. Of course he would.

After dinner, he gave me a tour of his house. The ex took a lot of things, so the furnishings were pretty sparse, but she managed to leave several photos of them that were still out. I didn't understand why in the world he would want that reminder displayed, but it wasn't any of my business so I didn't say anything. He had a nice yard with a large patio, swimming pool, and hot tub. We changed into our bathing suits, shared a bottle of wine in the hot tub, and talked the night away. What a great way to spend the evening. And true to his word, he was a complete gentleman – what a pleasant surprise.

Chapter 18

"I just wanted to drop you a note letting you know you're on my mind. ... You are going to get through this, and it will only make you that much stronger."

Handwritten by friend Leah

With New Year's coming up, Stephanie invited me to join her, her boyfriend, and their friends to go out for dinner and dancing. Fun! Alas, I have no date. I could ask Indiana or I could go alone. I'm sure he has plans, so I'll just tag along and have fun with whoever happens to be around. I'll wear my long brown wig with blonde highlights and dance the night away. A little bit of blonde will surely make things more lively! Turns out, we had a wonderful steak dinner but Steph's friends would not go dancing with us, so the three of us went by ourselves. We danced until midnight, rang in the New Year, and went home. Not terribly exciting ... but we have a new year ahead of us. That will be exciting!

My nose is constantly running now, but my skin is clear and my nails are strong and perfect. Who would have thought these treatments would actually improve some of my physical imperfections? I am enjoying those benefits and not experiencing any pain, diarrhea, constipation, or swollen ankles, as is common with many chemotherapy patients. I am, however, experiencing weight GAIN, which is NOT common with many chemotherapy patients. How is that possible? My body is being poisoned for crying out loud – how can I possibly weigh more every time I step on the scale? Inconceivable! I am not eating a lot, I am still working out, and I get plenty of rest, which I love because I get tired easily and can't wait to jump into bed. I am out like a light the moment my head hits the pillow – love that!

I just found out that my last treatment will be on April 12, 2006. Woohoo! Stephanie suggested that we go to Puerto Vallarta over Memorial Day weekend to celebrate her birthday and my being cancer free. I couldn't agree more! Then we'll go to San Diego in July to celebrate Grandma's 90th birthday and to Stillwater in October to celebrate the other Grandma's 90th birthday. We will definitely have numerous milestones to celebrate this year!

I've been thinking about Indiana and wondering how he is. Did they have fun in Mexico? Three hot single guys, are you kidding me? I can only imagine. I hope he isn't mortified when he sees me. I'm still the same person, but I look very different. Guess we'll see.

Bathrobe Boy

I thought Arizona was the same person I had known all these years, but I soon experienced another side of him I just didn't understand. Since my first visit to his home, the next two months were filled with fun! We spent the weekend in San Diego visiting my family – he was courteous and everyone liked him; he came to Chicago to wine, dine, and dance with my friends – he was generous and everyone liked him; I flew to Arizona and we hosted a St. Patrick's Day party for his friends and family – he was a gracious host and had a lot of female friends flitting around. I'm not a big fan of a bunch of flirtatious girls bouncing around, but they were his friends.

Much to my surprise, at that party, he introduced me to a gal who used to live in Chicago. Being the small world that it is, we quickly discovered that we both worked at the same company for awhile. Within moments of meeting, she said, "Aren't you the woman that (Pig Boy!) cheated on by taking another woman to Italy on vacation?"

I screamed, "WHAT?!!" as my hands flew up in the air then down to clutch my heart. My eyes popped out, my head must have spun around ... I was having a stroke! I had never seen this person before, yet she seemed to know intimate details of one of the most horrible events in my life. Who told?? Outrageous!! My mind and heart were racing ... how humiliating to know that probably everyone in the company knew about that ridiculous event. I'm sure they got a good laugh at my expense! EVIL.

Needless to say, I was dumbfounded and stood rooted to the floor blinking at her with my mouth hanging open, my shoulders slumped, and my hands still clutching my heart. An eternity later while everyone was staring at me in silence, I became conscious, shook my head to clear my thoughts, closed my mouth, stood up straight and laughed out loud. Ha! "Well, that was five long years ago – nobody cares. Bygones!" I turned around and walked out of the room. Unbelievable.

The next day, we went out with some of my friends who were visiting the sunshine state. Arizona was withdrawn, moody, and unsociable. He made a terrible impression, and they all wondered what I was doing with such a drip. I'd never seen him behave that way before. Everyone is entitled to a bad mood now and then – no big deal.

Shortly after arriving back in Chicago, I was laid off from my job. I knew it was coming, so Arizona and I had been discussing our future. Do we continue dating long distance or do we take a leap of faith and move me into his home and start a new life together? Not one to let the grass grow under my feet, I started packing my bags and searching for a new job in Arizona. The following week, I flew out for an interview, flew back to Chicago, and loaded clothes and a few personal things in my car. Stephanie took a week's vacation, and we drove across the country to begin my next adventure. Fun ... I was so excited and couldn't wait to get there!

About a mile away from the house, I called to let him know we were almost there. No answer. Hm ... wonder where he was?? Surely he was as excited about my arrival as I was! We pulled into the circular drive and parked the car. We made it! As we walked toward the front door, he stepped out wearing a striped bathrobe, phone to his ear and leered at us. With no smile, no hello, no hug ... he put his hand over the mouthpiece, looked around at the neighbor's houses, and said, "You're not going to leave your car there to unpack. What if it leaks oil on the driveway? Pull around to the garage." He promptly turned around, started talking on the phone again, went inside and closed the door.

Huh? I looked at Stephanie in puzzlement. What time is it? Why is he wearing a bathrobe in the middle of the day? Why isn't he welcoming us to his home? Why is he being an ass? He works from the house occasionally, so clearly that is what he is doing today. That's fine – he's obviously busy. I moved the car to the other side of the house and started unloading through the garage. Stephanie and I carried in load after load while Arizona stayed on the phone in his office. I was perfectly happy putting away all of my things in the huge walk-in closet and thinking of how much I was going to love living in a hot climate with no more winter!

Shortly after getting the car unloaded, Bathrobe Boy got off the phone, and we gave Stephanie the grand tour. As I entered each room and flipped on the lights so she could see, he promptly shut off the lights and said, "Clearly, you don't pay the bills here – keep the lights off during peak energy hours." Who is this guy? When did he become such a cheap ass? What's this about peak energy hours? Stephanie and I exchanged glances but didn't say anything – he was acting very strangely. We finished the tour and went outside to the patio for a drink. Much to my dismay, they both had a smoke. Aaah!! I hate cigarettes. So much for his quitting that nasty habit.

The rest of the week, Stephanie and I enjoyed shopping, soaking up sun by the pool, making dinner at the house, playing cards and dominoes, and going to movies. Out of my presence, she had a little chat with Bathrobe Boy about his attitude. "What's your damn problem?" He had no excuse other than being overwhelmed by our arrival and worrying about the increased cost ... AS IF we used so much electricity that he couldn't afford to pay the bill. He just needs to calm down. She assured him that I would get a job very soon and would help pay the bills. Actually, I should have had that conversation with him myself, but I didn't. I just kept my mouth shut and enjoyed Stephanie's company.

At the end of the week, we drove Stephanie to the airport, and I started to panic. What would I do without her? He still wasn't being nice to me, and I barely knew how to deal with him like that ... I was going to miss her so much. I wasn't ready to be on my own with such a cheap ass crab. I cried and hugged her, wishing she could stay. She was beside herself not wanting to leave me alone with him, but what could we do? Everything was going to be fine. Without her as my witness, no one would believe what a creep Bathrobe Boy was being to me, and I couldn't believe this was the life I had chosen. Now what?!

I had decided to make the best of it, so I put on a happy face and focused on the future. We spent the rest of the weekend fishing on a lake and swatting bugs. I had the joy of sitting in a little boat behind Bathrobe Boy watching him smoke, drink beer and attempt to catch fish. We talked about life, our goals, and our dreams. We both wanted children, but he made a comment I will never forget.

He said, "I'm concerned about you bearing my child because I don't want him to be stupid." Excuse me? I was sure I must not have heard him correctly.

I spouted incredulously, "WHAT did you just say?"

He totally back-peddled and tried to squirm out of it, but those words rang through my head over and over, and I just could not believe it. EVIL. I was so amazed by his ridiculous comment and the fact that he would even think that, I couldn't even speak. I had no response. No wonder he thinks I'm stupid. I should have clocked him, turned the boat over, swam to shore, and driven away right then, but I didn't. I had to pick my battles, so I let that slide. I actually let it slide! We sat in silence for the rest of the afternoon. My thoughts turned to getting a job, making new friends, and learning my way around. Again, this was the path I had chosen ... I could do it!

Chapter 19

*"We are so sorry you have to go through this and
are so glad Steph is close by to help and support you.
Please know that you are in our prayers."*
Handwritten by Aunt Pam

This being a new year, I decided to go to church to give thanks for my life. As I slid into an empty row and sat on the hard pew by myself, reflecting on the past few years and wondering what my future held, I looked around at the congregation. I was surrounded by happy young couples holding hands, parents fussing with their children, and older couples sitting shoulder-to-shoulder in silent contentment. Suddenly, my stomach knotted and my heart began to ache as I became overwhelmed with feeling empty, alone and very sad. I couldn't blink back the tears fast enough.

Would I ever share my world with someone? Having made a lifetime of bad choices, I now sit here by myself in a stocking cap with only whisps of hair underneath, no eyebrows, four eyelashes ... no amount of skillfully applied makeup seems to help. I look like a tired, shriveled 80-year-old man. Who could possibly love me when I look like this? How will I recover from this? Will I ever have a family? Am I destined to be alone? Overcome with even more sadness, self-pity, and an aching heart, my tears flowed and would not stop. I sobbed and blew my nose. Apparently I was no longer sitting alone, as a lady next to me put her arm around me, gave me a hug, and said, "God loves you." I could only nod and blink while streams of tears ran down my face and dripped onto my coat. I blinked and swallowed, prayed, and took deep calming breaths, trying desperately to change my thoughts into something positive, but I could not stop the flow -- my face had become a faucet. Finally, when all my tissues were soggy and useless, I knew I had to get a grip and snap out of it.

Why the tears? I guess I was feeling sorry for myself – what a pitiful, sad life I have created. I want a doting husband; I want a charming family. Two rows in front of me was a family with six amazingly well behaved children. Behind them was a family with two most likely adopted kids. Then I noticed several single women and a few overweight men – all sitting alone. Doomed. I really don't want to be alone the rest of my life, and it just makes me terribly sad to realize my choices put me in this predicament. No life is perfect or always happy, I know that. What can I do? I have read all the relationship self-help guides:

- *The Rules*
- *Men Are From Mars, Women Are From Venus*
- *In the Meantime – Finding Yourself and the Love You Want*
- *Rebuilding … When Your Relationship Ends*
- *Ten Stupid Things Women Do To Mess Up Their Lives*
- *Why Men Love Bitches*
- *When Love Goes Wrong*
- *He's Just Not That Into You*

None of these things have worked for me. OK, maybe some of them have actually helped me get through some rough patches. And my life certainly isn't horrible … I love my condo and love that no one eats all my cookies or drinks all my milk. No one is splashing water on my mirror, dribbling pee on my floor, or leaving the hair dryer plugged in after all. Even so, it would be wonderful to be loved by someone and to have someone to love. Gram called the other day, and she's so lonely without Gramps. My heart aches for her, too. What IS a girl to do? If you're lucky enough for life to go on, you suck it up and make the most of it doing whatever you want to do! The only person limiting me is ME. That's good news.

Camping

Therefore, I had to make the most of my choice to move in with Bathrobe Boy, who had his daily routine of getting up at the crack of dawn, putting on his ugly, too-small-for-his-belly-

striped bathrobe, making a pot of coffee, and walking outside for a morning smoke ... wonder when he is going to quit?? He could either work from home or go into the office a few miles down the road. Regardless of where he chose to work each day, when I got up, I took the dog for a walk around the neighborhood and got some exercise and fresh air. Beautiful!

After Stephanie was gone, I got busy! On Monday, I washed and waxed my car, went grocery shopping, had an interview with a recruiter, did laundry, cleaned house, pulled weeds and made dinner. I was then told NOT to do laundry, use the oven, or run the vacuum during peak energy hours. Is that right? Well ok then, I will simply pull weeds, swim in the pool and lay in the sun. No housekeeping duties ... works for me!

On Tuesday, I had a 9 a.m. interview, pulled weeds, went swimming and laid in the sun. On Wednesday, I did more job research, pulled weeds, went swimming and laid in the sun. On Thursday, I received a rejection letter in the mail, pulled weeds, went swimming and laid in the sun. What a life! I enjoyed pulling weeds and lounging; however, I really did want to find work, and Bathrobe Boy was hounding me to pound the pavement. Fortunately, he went turkey hunting all weekend, so I went hiking with friends.

During week two after Stephanie left, on Monday I submitted more job applications, changed my address on everything, and set up a new email account. On Tuesday, I applied to be the Executive Assistant to the CEO and CFO of a dialysis center, interviewed with them on Wednesday morning, and was offered the job that afternoon. Piece of cake! I celebrated that evening with a girlfriend from Chicago who was in town for a conference. Bathrobe Boy thought I should have been at home with him, not out celebrating with a friend, so he was mad at me instead of being happy and supportive. However, he softened and decided that we were going to celebrate by going camping and fishing all weekend in the Blue Ridge Mountains. Oh boy ... can we? That was certainly not my idea of a celebration, but I didn't have an acceptable alternative to suggest.

Friday morning, the sun came up to usher in a hot, sunny, beautiful day. We packed the truck with camping gear, food and drinks, hitched up the boat, grabbed the dog and drove up into the mountains. After quite a drive, we arrived at the lake, unpacked the truck, loaded up the boat with our supplies, and traveled a good mile or so up a river to the campsite. Solitude. No other campers around, no running water -- just nature, a boat and a tent. It wasn't so bad I guess. We hauled everything up a hill to a little clearing, set up camp, gathered firewood, and went fishing. I might have held a pole, I don't recall. I do not enjoy fishing, but I was fine with rowing, catching some sun, and swatting bugs. We talked a little, but mostly just sat with our own thoughts. I did have the pleasure of turning my back when he lit up a smoke. Gross.

After what seemed like hours, we paddled back to camp and dined on franks and beans, which produced a delightfully musical evening – is every guy amused by farts? Please. Shortly after the sun had dropped into the lake, we let the campfire burn out since the sky opened up and poured buckets of rain on it. All of a sudden, the temperature dropped to really cold. He never told me it was going to be 100 degrees during the day and zero at night. Who knew?! With no hot shower available, I just snuggled down into my sleeping bag wearing my sweatshirt and the grime of the day and went to sleep. Glorious.

As usual, he and the dog woke up with the sun, started a pot of coffee, and filled the air with smoke. I decided to forego fishing and stayed behind to spruce up the camp site, gather firewood and pine cones, sit in the sun and read my book. The day passed peacefully and leisurely with thoughts of starting a new adventure on Monday.

When he came back to camp, we started preparing dinner, and he made an announcement.

"We are having green apple martinis with dinner so that you will loosen up and tell me what's on your mind."

"Is that right?! Be careful what you wish for, mister," I thought to myself. However, I chuckled and said, "Great – cheers!"

We proceeded to drink, eat and play cards. As the evening wore on, it got colder and colder and started to snow!

"You didn't tell me it was going to snow."

Clearly, I was unprepared as I only had a sweatshirt, so he graciously gave me his coat all the while whining that I didn't pack well. Having had my first martini, I was finding my voice.

"Whose fault is that?! I have never camped in a tent in these mountains, and I had no idea to expect rain or snow. Thanks for the warning, by the way. YOU should have told me the temperature dropped to freezing at night and that I should bring a parka – how on earth would I know that?"

He claimed, "Everybody knows that ... it's common knowledge."

Posh! It surely is not. Down went another martini encouraging me to feel free to speak my mind, just like he wanted. My thoughts were swirling close to the surface, and I was getting braver with each green swallow.

Next thing I knew, he planted himself in front of me and defiantly lit a cigarette. He took a big puff and blew the smoke right in my face. As I'm sure he predicted, I flipped out! I despise seeing him with a cancer stick dangling from his lips, and it pushed me over the edge … I was ready to blow!

As he wished, I launched into him shouting, "You know how I hate smoking! It's a disgusting habit and you are beyond rude to continue smoking in front of me when you know how I feel about it! Before I moved out here, you promised to quit … you're not even trying!"

With the snow coming down harder than ever, he ducked into the tent, and I stomped in after him continuing to rant and rave and flail my arms. Isn't this what he wanted after all?! He provoked me! By that point, I was incensed with fury and yelling about all the ridiculous things I had put up with for the past three weeks. He got right back in my face so close that I could have wrapped my hands around his thick neck and choked him (another wishful choking episode!), but I had enough sense to merely kick him in the shin. And WHACK! With his whole arm, he hit me across the chest and knocked me down to the ground. In stunned shock, I sat there and glared up at him.

"How DARE you hit me!"

"You kick me, I'm going to hit you."

Again, I was speechless. Glaring at each other, neither of us moved a muscle. I thought … who the hell is this man? Not somebody I want in my life for one more minute.

Immediately sober, I knew that I was leaving for Chicago the moment we got back to the house. Think fast ... what to do — what to do? I'm stuck. Clearly, I couldn't get myself back, as I was stranded in the middle of nowhere without any way to leave on my own — I am at his mercy. Unfortunate!

I stood up without saying a word, and he screamed, "GET OUT of my tent and give me my coat!" I threw the coat at him and stepped out into the snow wearing only my sweatshirt while he and the dog zipped me out. What a creep ... this is unbelievable and certainly NOT part of my plan. Now what?

Chapter 20

Oh my Dear God, I don't know whether to laugh or to keep crying. I have never looked or felt so hideous in all my life. When I look in the mirror, and I can only glance for a moment, I see ugly, pale, and old. Depressing. At first I looked like a Sunday school teacher I had in high school, whom I had seen years after graduating as he was suffering from cancer treatments, sitting in the church pew a few rows in front of me – pale, bald, frail – a shell of the man I once admired so much. He looked sad and pitiful, and it broke my heart to see him that way. That vision is etched in my memory.

At second glance in the mirror, I'm reminded of a baby bird I almost stepped on once. During a storm, the newborn was blown out of its nest and left to die in the grass. My heart ached for the poor baby, as it had not a single feather, not even a little fluff of down, its tiny eyes bulging out of its head, skin so transparent you could see its little blue veins. It didn't have a chance at life, so small and helpless, taken away from its family by a gust of wind. I saw it before I stepped on it, thank God. I would have shuddered for days had I crushed it – like the time I accidentally stepped on a little frog with my bare foot – I screamed out loud! Or when you hit a possum on the road – they are disgusting stupid varmints, but I can't stand the sound or sight of running over any animal. It takes days for the image and sound to go away. My reflection is both sad and pitiful. Hope nobody runs over me today.

I'm a Leo – I'm supposed to have piles of gorgeous, thick, wonderful hair. And I did. Without it, I feel exposed and ugly. No wonder animals slink away to hide after you shave their hair off. Now I know exactly how they feel.

After five treatments, I was still feeling fairly energetic, still working, still going to the gym, and still losing hair every day. Enough was enough. My most wonderfully supportive girlfriend, Debbie, came over last night with enthusiasm, a smile, and borrowed shears to shave my head. I would not consider going to a salon, so she agreed to help me out while being as cheerful as possible.

In the bathroom, I sat on the pot facing the mirror, and she got right to work. In disbelief, I watched her remove the last bit of hair I had and wow … could I be any uglier? The buzz didn't take long. She asked me how I felt. At the time, I was too mortified to feel much of anything. I didn't want to have any feelings because I knew they would only be sad and make me cry. She did me a huge favor, and I didn't want to cry or make her feel bad in any way. Being brave and strong, I got up, swept up my hair, and left the bathroom. No big deal. I put on a scarf and almost looked like a normal human being. I even almost felt less ugly.

But then I couldn't help it, the tears began to fall and I couldn't be strong anymore. I cried and cried while she held me. I couldn't hold in my grief any longer -- the heartache, the sadness, the unfairness of it all was too much … I sobbed until I was exhausted. Debbie remained strong and patiently waited for me to calm down.

Why am I so upset? It's just hair – yet it's really so much more than that. It was my identity, a source of pride and joy. People don't recognize me in my wigs until I speak to them, and they recognize my voice. Losing your hair is a huge sense of loss – HUGE. And I know it's OK to feel despair. At the same time, I realize I am going to be OK. I'm not going to die – I will survive and live my life. I no longer have to sweep up hair. I can start fresh when it grows back. I'm fine. I will be just fine. In fact, I am in the process of being cured. I can envision a light at the end of this tunnel.

Fire

As I stood in the snow on that mountain, facing the campfire, hunkered down into my sweatshirt, I could see the light at the end of that nightmare as well. I had no watch to tell the time. I knew it was night because it was pitch black. The moon was directly overhead – that meant it was late, but I had no idea how late.

What am I doing? I'm not a Girl Scout or a camper ... and this is not my idea of a good time. Are there animals out here? Bears? Coyotes? Monkeys? You never know what is waiting to attack you! I should be very afraid, but I just stood there shivering, staring at the dying flames, and wondering how long I had to wait for sunrise.

Yet the whole fiasco of the past three weeks almost made me laugh out loud. I was too numb to be angry. I stood as close to the fire as I could to keep warm, but I needed more fuel. I had burned all the firewood and pinecones I had gathered earlier that day. I grabbed what I could find – in went a rug, a roll of paper towels, my book, a loaf of bread, the chips, the potatoes, the carton of eggs, and then the alcohol. Whatever I could easily toss in amused me for awhile. Besides, we won't be needing it! I want to leave in the morning ASAP! If we have no food or drinks, we will have to head back pronto. For fear of his reaction, I didn't want to burn anything too valuable, so I quickly ran out of heat. The moon had moved behind the trees ... how much time had passed? Just what am I going to do now??

As if he sensed my frustration, I heard a voice from inside the tent say, "You can come in."

AS IF. I stood frozen in my tracks and remained silent.

Again he said, "You've been out there long enough, you can come in."

I sure didn't want to, but I was exhausted and cold and didn't know what else to do. I unzipped the doorway, climbed over him and the dog, and crawled into my sleeping bag shoes and all. I fell asleep knowing that they would get up in a few hours with the sun. Morning can't get here fast enough!

I kept waking up waiting for the day to begin. Finally, the sun came up but guess who decided to sleep in? Honestly. I bolted out of the tent trying to make enough noise to get some action from the sleeping dog and his master – no such luck. I went in search of a hole in the ground and some big leaves since we had no toilet paper left – ha! When I came back to camp, the boys were still asleep or pretending to be. Apparently, he can't function without his too-small-ugly-striped bathrobe. I sat down, my back against a tree, looked out at the steam rising off the lake while the sun continued to rise and waited.

At long last, the beast emerged. I had nothing to say, so I simply sat and waited. He looked around and said, "Where is everything?"

"I don't know what you're talking about."

"The rug, the food in the cooler, the paper products?"

I gave my icy confession, "I burned them last night when I ran out of firewood. How did you expect me to stay warm?" (Moron)

Assuming he would be outraged enough to pack up and go, I was surprised when he grabbed his fishing rod and headed toward the boat. He turned around and said, "Don't you dare touch one more thing ... not one thing!" He and the dog hopped in the boat and off they went. Inconceivable! I guess he showed me.

I didn't do a single thing until they came back. I didn't have a watch, but it sure felt like several hours later. I had no food, no drink, and I did nothing. Did they go find breakfast somewhere? I didn't ask. I refused to look at him. He started packing up the gear, so I got up to help. He barked, "Sit down and stay out of the way and touch nothing."

Fine. He can do it all by himself. I watched him make trip after trip down to the boat. When he had it all loaded, he grabbed the dog, hopped in and he would have left me if I didn't leap into the boat.

How could I have thought I loved or even knew this man well enough to move my life out to the desert for him? I'm a risk taker, but I'm not a complete fool. He's selfish, rude, mean, cheap and certainly doesn't love me. Magically, I had already detached myself from him emotionally. I simply didn't care. I wasn't mad or upset, I just wanted to leave.

As soon as we landed at the loading dock, he got the truck and we unloaded the boat – not a word was exchanged. When everything was in its place, we buckled in and drove down the mountain. Thanks to my careful planning, I had no food or drink all day, and I didn't ask for any. However, he pulled into an ice cream shop for a snack. Naturally, he didn't ask me if I wanted anything. While he was inside, I ran to the hamburger shop across the street and got my own food. I beat him back to the truck so he couldn't leave me stranded and watched him and the dog share an ice cream cone. Nasty. I rolled my eyes and looked out the side window so they were out of my sight. I couldn't wait to leave.

An eternity later, we pulled into the garage at the house. I threw the door open, jumped out, and immediately started packing. He was kind enough to pull out my clothes from the coat closet in the living room so I wouldn't forget them. Good to know we were both on board with my departure.

As I was making trips from the closet through the bathroom to the garage, I noticed he was taking a shower. That in itself was not unusual or surprising after a weekend in the woods. The odd thing was seeing him soaping up the dog in the shower. Doesn't seem right. Since the dog sleeps in the bed, I guess that showering together makes sense. At least he was being kind to someone. Go figure.

On my last pass back into the closet, I happened to glance in the mirror. I barely recognized myself! My long hair was pulled into a ponytail all weekend, so my entire face was exposed to the elements – sun, fire, rain and snow – and I had 2nd degree burns and blisters on my forehead, chin, cheeks and nose. I had no idea! Since I hadn't seen a mirror or washed my face for days, I didn't notice and it didn't hurt. Ghastly!! I can't believe he didn't say anything. How on earth is that possible? I stopped, washed my face, and put on some moisturizer before taking the last load to the car. I was actually excited about going back to Chicago, and I couldn't get out of there fast enough.

As I walked out of the closet for the last time, he droned, "Leave money for the things you burned."

You've got to be kidding. That's all he had to say? EVIL. I wanted to hate him for being such a cheap ass uncaring bastard, but I didn't have the time or the energy. I wrote a check and left it on the dresser. He could buy cigarettes with it for all I cared. The last thing I saw was the too-small-ugly-striped bathrobe hanging limply on its hook. Wish I could have thrown that in the fire!

I stayed with friends that night who couldn't believe the condition of my face or the ridiculous tale of the weekend. At 8 a.m. the next morning, I called my new employer to say sorry, I won't be coming in today or ever — I'm moving back to Chicago. I felt terrible about it, but I really had no choice. If those three weeks were any indication of how my life would have been in Arizona, I was on the fastrack to misery. Been there, done that. No thanks ... I'm outta here!

As soon as I got on the road, my cell phone rang. It was him. Not answering. I have nothing to say nor do I give a sand-covered-cat's-crap about what he thinks. My phone rang every hour. Still not answering. To my glorious personal satisfaction, I drove myself all the way to Chicago in two days without so much as a single doubt that I was going the right way. With the radio for company, I couldn't have been happier during that trip singing and calling family, friends, and my recruiter. Get ready ... I'm coming home! By the time I got back to my old apartment and my roommate (she had to move her stuff out of my room so I could move back in!), my face was full of scabs, but my heart was free, and I was ready for a fresh start. Thank God.

Chapter 21

"The Lord is near to all who call on him ...
Pray hard! We will, too."

Card from friends Pam and Dave

My work friends have been amazingly supportive throughout this ordeal. Every other week when I have a treatment and need to eat before I go, we get together in the office kitchen for lunch. Sometimes they buy lunch, and we enjoy Thai, Italian, or Chinese. Sometimes they make it, and we enjoy Mexican, Italian or American. Regardless, it is a delicious, nutritious, thoughtful send off. They really make me feel special with their extra effort and by taking the time to share a meal with me. Fortunately, the only work I miss is a half-day Wednesday when I go to the hospital. And even more fortunately, my trip to the hospital is only 15 minutes from the office. Some people travel for hours. I know ... I am so lucky.

I have been experiencing body aches lately, especially in my right elbow. The nurse says it is from the chemo, so we'll use the left arm today for treatment #6. I see patients of all types – young, old, men, women – in the cancer center waiting room, and I wonder how they're doing. Are they alone? Do they have supportive family and friends? How do they feel? Is their insurance covering the costs? Of course I don't ask anyone, I just mind my own business. If anyone starts to ask me about how I'm feeling, the tears well up in my eyes and I cry. Even though I'm getting along fine, I can't help it. This is the most traumatic, emotional, anxiety-filled experience of my life – more than a wedding or a divorce – but then I haven't lost a child. That pain is unimaginable to me. I don't know how I would handle that.

This evening I had the pleasure of Supper Club, which is a group of 5 or 6 of my girlfriends who gather once a month at a new restaurant in the city. We have a never-ending supply of fabulous places to try! We enjoy great food, good wine, and each other's company as we tell stories and catch up on our lives. After I gave my emotional update, I learned the mother-in-law of one of the gals was diagnosed with breast cancer and another's fiancé has a brain tumor. His treatments are so severe that he is very, very sick and can't work. My heart aches for them. While this doesn't diminish my cancer, it certainly puts things in perspective for me. I am *so* thankful and *so* lucky, as I know I will survive. Health is a precious gift that we absolutely must protect, and I am constantly amazed at the number of people who continually abuse their bodies with alcohol, drugs, and other bad habits when they know what it's doing to them. I don't get that.

Introduce New York

After all, I had just lost one big, bad habit. Happy and excited to be back in Chicago after my grueling camping trip, I never looked or felt better! My facial scabs disappeared leaving a glowing tan, and I managed to lose 10 pounds during that fateful month. When I was married and proudly expressed to my husband that I had lost some weight, he would gleefully say — turn around, you'll find it. Evil! However, at this moment, if I turn around, I will not find it … Yippee!!

Not one to let the grass grow under my feet, I jumped right into action. The very day after I arrived back home, I had lunch with a friend and then interviewed with a recruiter. That evening, my roommate and I celebrated my return by going out for an expensive dinner and dancing until midnight at our favorite stomping grounds. Wow, it was GREAT to be back!

The following day I had a job interview, unpacked my car, repacked my suitcase and zoomed down state to visit the Kettles for the weekend. Mom and I shopped, ate, and worked in the yard.

I was going to miss pulling weeds every day. Pleeeaaase! When I returned to the city on Monday, I lined up several interviews for the week and started a temp job. After a month of no income, I needed to make some money. Chicago certainly has more opportunity than the desert.

I had also been fielding calls from Too-Small-Ugly-Striped-Bathrobe Boy. When I think of him, that vision is what comes to mind ... it almost makes me laugh! The memory that does make me laugh is the night he strutted out into the living room in a t-shirt I had bought for him and plopped down on the couch for a night of television. I'm pretty sure he was proving that the shirt was too small, but I couldn't get past the dangling nads ... when did it become acceptable to lounge on the couch with no underwear or shorts?! Excuse me ... unacceptable!

Since I truly had detached myself from him emotionally, listening to his revelations and excuses did not move me. He insisted on seeing me and wouldn't let it go ... he was so sorry, had made huge mistakes, and would do whatever it took to win me back. He needed to see me. Fine – I couldn't imagine what he could possibly say that would ever make me want to be with him again.

Much to the dismay of everyone else in my life, I agreed to have dinner with him. After being such a rude tight wad during the past month, he was suddenly generous with cards, gifts, and dinner. He asked about my friends and family. Low and behold, he had quit smoking. Not only that, he was willing to pack my bags, load the truck, and drive me back. This amazing offer was from the same man who couldn't bother to get dressed the day I arrived at his front door and turned his back on me. I watched his face as he spoke, his mouth spewing meaningless words. My spirit was hovering over the table observing the transaction, but my mind was numb. My heart was frozen, and I had no interest in reconciling. He couldn't buy my love with gifts, regardless of how thoughtful. He may have quit smoking during the past two weeks, but it won't last. I didn't believe in him or trust him. I didn't hate him; in fact, I felt utterly indifferent. The apologies, the pleas, the tears ... it was all too little, too late. I had checked out.

By the middle of the following week, I had checked into my next adventure! I accepted a full-time position at a software company and started making new friends. That Friday night, a small group invited me out to happy hour. The instigator of the evening was a mystery and an interesting man to observe. He smoothly moved around the office, confident and unsure at the same time, unassumingly checking things out. Did he think he was inconspicuous? Hardly! He was clearly not from the Midwest. He stood tall with perfect posture and broad shoulders, wore his jeans very well, had an expensive watch and shoes, smelled good and had a shockingly sexy, deep voice. What was his role here? What was his story? He was carrying around photos of his infant son and showing them to people. I didn't see a wedding ring ... I was definitely intrigued!

A cluster of us went to an establishment across the street from the office and had a few drinks. He clearly enjoyed being the leader of the pack and quickly took charge of the group. He was full of stories, so it didn't take long to learn that he had made big bucks from a company he took public on Wall Street in New York, had lived large in Manhattan, and had traveled the world doing business. He introduced himself to everyone as the guy from New York ... he was very proud of what he had accomplished there and was reluctantly living in Chicago – he hates Chicago. The other bad news ... he smokes. Aaahhhh! It didn't matter – a guy like that would have no interest in a small town girl like me anyway.

Reduced to a smaller group, we all piled into his beautiful, luxurious BMW and moved our happy hour to another location. We consumed more drinks and dinner and shared more stories. By 10 pm, three of us were left, and he wanted to know a fun place to go. By all means, we drove to Rush & Division, and I introduced him to my favorite stomping grounds. At that point, he and I were on our own. The place was packed, as usual. He slipped a generous tip to the bouncer and magically, we had a table. Awesome!

We ordered martinis and ended up sharing our table with another couple. We drank, talked and danced the night away. He was a great dancer and so much fun ... this is just what I needed after the Arizona disaster of no fun at all! He was amazed that I was keeping up with him and asked where we should go next, probably thinking I would say that was enough. Instead, I introduced him to another old favorite of mine ... we drank and danced until 4 a.m. Ok, Ok, time to go home. We made plans to go out the following evening to celebrate Stephanie's birthday ... won't she be surprised!

Chapter 22

"You're a SuperStar! ... That's what you are!"
Card from my friend Mary

Just finished another workout with my personal trainer. We have two more sessions left, and I'm elated ... I'm also pooped! I signed up for this torture because I had a vision in the forefront of my mind that this investment of time and money would yield a fabulous body. My shape would morph into sculpted calves, sleek thighs, tight buns, shapely arms, and six-pack abs. Did that materialize? Let's see ... actually, I look the same as the day I started sans the hair. After all these hours of working out, how is that even possible? Oh well, I tried but now I'm tired and my arms hurt. I'm going home.

I love my home, and I love being home. It's warm, cozy, colorful, peaceful and all mine! And I just got a new bedspread, pillows, shams, and sheets plus a beautiful cabinet to organize all the miscellaneous stuff that had no place. Now everything has a place and everything is in its place without an inch to spare ... gives me great satisfaction. I love it! And I can't wait to jump into bed, snuggle down under my new sheets, and think about my day tomorrow. As a matter of fact, tomorrow I am having lunch with Indiana. I can't imagine what he is going to think when he sees me now with my red wig, drawn on eyebrows and four eyelashes. Guess we'll see!

New York Says He's Evil

Guess I was excited to see how surprised Stephanie would be when I brought New York with me to her birthday party. She was annoyed that she wasted a week of her vacation moving me to

Arizona, only to have me back less than a month later. However, unlike Arizona, New York was fun, generous, entertaining and interesting. Just like I thought, she was surprised and she liked him. So did all of her girlfriends. What's not to like?!

New York and I hit the fast track on fun while we explored Chicago together. He soon learned that The Windy City was not only fun, it was easy compared to The Big Apple. It was easy to get a dinner reservation; it was easy to get tickets to a show; it was easy to get into any club; it was easy to catch a cab; it was easy to drive to work; it was easy to make new friends. Everything was so easy that I was as certain he would grow to love Chicago, as I was certain that he would grow to love me.

He introduced me to some of his friends, and I introduced him to a few of mine. We enjoyed fine dining and dancing the nights away. We went to musicals, concerts, street festivals, Cubs games, and dinner cruises. We ate, danced, drank, and laughed. We had no cares and no troubles ... life was great!

Late one night when we arrived at his place after another exhausting night on the town, he chuckled and said, "You know, I'm Evil."

"HA!" I laughed out loud. "You are not Evil – what are you talking about?" In all seriousness, he told me again.

"You'll see ... I am Evil."

I couldn't imagine what he was talking about. All he had been to that point was fantastic. Whatever – I dismissed the words as preposterous. But then I started paying attention, and little snippettes of his real life started to surface.

In fact, one thing New York insisted upon was that our relationship remain Top Secret to the general population at our office since we did work at the same place. Why? I didn't see what the big deal was. After all, we were with co-workers the first night we went out. However, I am not a fan of office gossip, so with the exception of a few confidants, my lips were sealed.

Then one evening while hanging out at his place, the phone rang. He leaped to the phone, looked at me with steely green eyes, and placed his index finger across his lips. In a deep hushed whisper, he said, "Sssshhh, don't say a word," as if whomever was calling could already hear his voice. My eyebrows flew up, the corners of my mouth drew down, my wide eyes blinked, my heart clinched, and my mouth clamped shut but my ears blossomed into megaphones. I was about to learn a secret!

He answered the phone, paced around the room while talking and listening, and did not glance at me. He knew I was holding my breath, not wanting to miss hearing a word. Who was it? What did they want? Was this someone he cared about? Was it an old girlfriend? He was asking about his son. Ah, it must be his ex. We don't talk about that situation – he says it has nothing to do with me, and I don't need to know. For now, I respect that. When he's ready, he'll tell me.

After the call, he was sullen and depressed. Clearly, he missed his baby, who was only five months old. He didn't want to talk about it. I am his escape from that life. He didn't want me asking questions – again, it had nothing to do with me. Huh? As new friends spending a lot of time together, I wanted to know what was going on in his life. I managed to learn that his ex was actually still his wife, but he preferred to place her in the ex category. Oh boy ... complication. This man was actually still married, even though

119

he did not consider himself to be. While I was a secret at work, clearly I was to remain a secret to the "ex" as well! Um, do I smell an evil rat? Not ready to let go of my new fun life over this minor detail, I decided to see how this changed things.

Chapter 23

"Times like these require extra patience and strength and you may be wondering how you'll ever manage. I don't have any easy answers, but I do have a lot of support to give whenever you need it."
Card from friends Shelly, Jim & Chase

I had lunch with Indiana today at *Wells on Wells,* one of my favorite lunch spots in Old Town. He's a handsome guy with a sexy, warm smile, and I could tell he was nervous. Can't blame him – I am a fairly intimidating hairless woman after all. Ha! He has been working out with a trainer and hasn't eaten junk food for six months. Wow ... that's huge for a man who is on the road all the time and loves French fries as much as he does! He's been hot and heavy on the dating scene, but I wonder if he is emotionally available yet. Are any of us really?

We spent an enjoyable hour together catching up on the last year-and-a-half. I'm amazed that it had been that long since we broke up. And actually, I am amazed that he even wanted to see me because I wasn't very nice to him back then. I often felt like he was comparing me to his ex, and believe me, I let him know in no uncertain terms that I cannot stand that and will not tolerate it. I might have even been unreasonable a time or two. Is that even possible? I could flip out right now just thinking about it! Why on earth would he consider subjecting himself to that again? Apparently, he is forgiving and far more patient than I.

Much to my relief, not once did he scrutinize how I looked. Not that he would ever say anything out loud anyway. As self-conscious as I was, I presented the same old cheerful Kelly I've always been. I kept thinking that if he saw me without the wig and make-up, he'd think he was having lunch with a bald old man. Not that there's anything wrong with bald old men -- I just don't want to be one!

Reflecting on the events that have brought me to this point in my life, now is a good time to be forward thinking and set some short-term goals. (Indiana claims to be a forward thinker who has let go of the past ... seriously? I'm skeptical.)

1. Become cancer free.
2. Grow my hair back.
3. Buy a two-bedroom/two-bath condo with a lake view, parking, and in-unit laundry (a gal must have priorities, you know).
4. Marry the love of my life and be very happy together.
5. Appreciate my good life ... I am SO lucky!

4th of July

Living the good life with New York, we decided to plan a big 4th of July bash and invite my friends and some of their friends. New York generously hosted at his place, catered the event, and provided a full bar. He had a few stipulations ... absolutely no one was allowed to use the bathroom in his bedroom and absolutely nothing was to be spilled on the carpet. Stephanie and I would make sure those rules were followed.

Our guests began arriving several hours before dark. They drank, munched, listened to music, and drank some more. A few of our younger guests were visiting from France and loved this American holiday. What's not to love? We had a spectacular view of the fireworks, loud music for singing and dancing, delicious food and free drinks!

As the evening wore on, food spilled off plates, drinks were sloshed on the floor, and the dancing was out of control – mostly by New York himself. Stephanie and I were trying frantically to keep everything cleaned up. One young Frenchman, nearly passed out in a chair, leaned over the coffee table and heaved the contents of his stomach all over it. Gross!! We drug him to the bathroom and

laid him in the tub while we cleaned up before New York noticed
the mess. However, every time I walked back into the living room,
New York was dirty dancing with someone crushed against the
wall, so he was oblivious. (Is he evil?!) I was clearly not amused.
Stephanie was not amused at being the babysitter and cleaning
crew. Enough – everybody out! Party over.

Stephanie and I did our best to leave no evidence of spillage
before we left. New York's eyes were glazed over, and he never
noticed a thing. Turns out his binge required an entire day in bed
to recover, and I doubt he even remembered anything that happened
during the entire evening. Magically, this started a pattern of
behavior that neither of us could tolerate. We'd go out – he would
smoke and drink too much – I would get seriously and obviously
annoyed – he would send me home in a huff – and he'd sleep away
the following day.

Quickly, our favorite stomping grounds turned into his
playground, and I was no longer welcome there. I can only speculate
what went on, but I guarantee it was not in my best interest. I sense
Evil. Surely this was a phase he was going through, and he'd soon
realize this crazy lifestyle could not be sustained. Weeks went by
when all would be fine, then we'd have a big, bad fight and break
up. We would get back together, but the pattern continued. We
eventually reached a compromise where he would go out with his
friends without me, and our time together would be quiet evenings
at home alone.

One day he sprang some news on me. He was going to Paris to
visit his "ex" and son for a week. Paris? One of the most beautiful
and romantic cities in the world? He might as well have stabbed
me. My imagination was running amuck, and my heart actually
broke. How could he do that? Why would he go there of all

places? He insisted that due to circumstances, Paris was the best location. Oh sure! Who wouldn't want an all-expense paid trip in a luxurious hotel on the Champs Elysees? The whole time he was gone, I was beside myself and absolutely sick to my stomach. I couldn't control how I felt any more than I could stop the trip from happening. Evil.

When he returned, I was an emotional, exhausted wreck. He was sullen and depressed and missed his son terribly. While he had nothing positive to say about the "ex," he couldn't believe the pain he felt in seeing his son, who didn't recognize him. By the time they got reacquainted, their visit was over. Brutal. As I looked past my own selfish feelings, I could see his pain ran far deeper than I could fathom. He needed some alone time, so Stephanie and I went to visit Grandma in Minnesota. I needed some cheering up!

Chapter 24

"More than anyone I know, you adapt to change, good or bad. This amazing quality will aide you on your new journey to recovery. Your strength will pull you through the tough times with a grace and resolve, together with the strength and love of your friends and family."

Handwritten from my friend Sally

Tomorrow is February 1, 2006. When I wake up in the morning, I need to remember to crawl off the end of the bed while chanting Rabbit-Rabbit-Rabbit. I had a dear friend back in the 80s named Molly who told me if I did that the first morning of every month, I would have good luck in my life. So far, I have not managed to remember this little trick until I am already in the shower! Even so, I've been pretty lucky in the grand scheme of things.

It is now officially the 1st of February. Rats! I woke up from a crazy dream and, as usual, forgot to crawl out the end of the bed. No luck for me. And as it turns out, no luck for Molly. She suffered from Alzheimer's disease for several years and has passed. She was a great friend and co-worker who used to peer at me through the plants between our cubes until I noticed her, and her desk was always covered with yellow sticky notes – much to her boss's dismay. She was a nut, and I think of her fondly every first day of the month.

Chemo #8 today – past half way! Today we will schedule the next round of scans to see if the cancer is gone. Let's hope so. I haven't been sleeping well, which is highly unusual for me. Also highly unusual, my fingernails are growing beautifully, and my complexion is as smooth and blemish-free as it has ever been. I had feared that all of these drugs being pumped into my body would absolutely tear me down, but they're not. I still don't feel sick, I still haven't lost my appetite (boo!), and I still have plenty of energy to work. Thankfully, I'm not depressed, miserable, sad or lonely. Who knew?!

Buy Condo

And in spite of all my heartache and drama because of New York, a glimmer of happiness shined in my life like a rainbow through the clouds. I bought my first home! It had everything I wanted … hardwood floors, fireplace, balcony, in-unit washer/ dryer, lots of closets, indoor parking, and a 10-minute walk to work. My friend Malissa helped me paint, and another friend Peter helped me tile a backsplash in the kitchen. I had purchased several pieces of original artwork painted by artist-friends, and I loved everything. Perfect!

I had been staying with New York during the transition from apartment to condo. One night after a work party where we pretended not to know each other (AS IF!), I went to his place alone and waited for him to come home. As hour after hour passed with no phone call and no burst through the front door, my blood started to boil. I declared that it was time for me to leave his rude, inconsiderate, self-serving, self-absorbed mopey evil ass. What could I expect from a man whose favorite book is "American Psycho" and whose favorite movie is "Jacob's Ladder." He was right – he is evil. Now I believe him, but surely my wholesome good influence would bring light into his life. Not.

In fact, New York has told me on more than one occasion that I have a dark side. He said I was the devil in disguise. Of course he would think that. A couple of times when we still dared to socialize together at our favorite stomping grounds, his flock of minions would scurry away like roaches when I approached the table. As I poured their drinks out onto the floor, I couldn't stop myself. After all, the devil made me do it.

In a flurry, I began packing his big, beautiful, luxurious car full of all my things. (Hm ... this is just another version of my Arizona nightmare.) Load after load, the doorman watched me move out. Trust me, door staff know everything. If I could have picked his brain for five minutes, I'm afraid what I would have learned! I don't want to know.

In my own peaceful home at last, I quickly became quite the entertainer by hosting a design-your-own purse party, wine tasting, dinner for friends, and my first Thanksgiving. From this year forward, I shall be the family Thanksgiving host.

The day after Thanksgiving, when everyone else is shopping, out come my Christmas decorations. My shopping has been done for a month! A dozen storage tubs full of decorations collected over the years replace everything that is normally adorning the place. While it takes hours and hours to complete the transformation, it's fabulously festive and cheerful!

I rang in the New Year with a few girlfriends. We each bought a new ball gown and got all dolled up hoping to meet Prince Charming by midnight. We enjoyed an evening of dinner, dancing, and drinking champagne at Navy Pier then treated ourselves to a night at the Drake Hotel. Prince Charming didn't find us, but crabby accusatory (what was I doing at a hotel?!) New York called to say Happy New Year. This is bound to be the best year ever!

Chapter 25

"Just a little note to let you know that you can count on our emotional
support during the difficult months ahead ...
we are so sorry that you are going
to have to deal with such an unfair illness.
We admire your courage and
positive attitude – it will be necessary."
Handwritten from friends Anne and Bob

My boss gave me a beautiful ring today made from Swarovski crystal beads as a thank you for working so hard lately. She's a thoughtful woman. Sure wish we could sell one of her listings. We work so hard to market her properties, and we do have a lot of showings. Buyers have so many options. Apparently, it is impossible for them to make a choice. It's absolutely exhausting, and I'm pooped.

Even though I wanted to go home and go to sleep, I went out for a delicious steak dinner tonight with Indiana. I can't figure him out. He obviously likes me, but he acts so nervous – like I'm judging what he wears, where he takes me, and every word he utters. Does he enjoy our dates? He almost has a look of dread ... as if any moment I'm going to freak out and throw my drink in his face and tell him to leave me alone! Poor fella. How horrible that I could make a good man worry about something so dreadful. Besides, I wouldn't dream of doing any such thing to him – but perhaps I was a little unpredictable when we dated a year-and-a-half ago, so he's a little on edge. Back then, I realize now, I was hypercritical and quick to snap when he said something I decided was inappropriate. Back then, I was torn between Good versus Evil... I just didn't know it. My perspective is different now.

Ravinia

After I moved into my wonderful new condo, I believed life was good! I practically skipped to work in the morning – loved not taking the bus. I joined the gym mid-way between my condo and the office and worked out during lunch or after work on the way home. Work was a breeze ... I had the privilege of planning parties, booking travel, and running errands or shopping for my boss. Was I lucky or what?! I certainly thought so until New York and I were on the outs. Then it was living torture going to that office. I wasn't nearly busy enough, and I could hear his deep voice laughing and talking a few cubes away – he absolutely taunted me, and I couldn't stand it.

Fortunately, he was relocated to another area, and I only saw him occasionally in passing. Since we "didn't know each other," he was easy to avoid. However, ignoring each other never lasted long. We talked and argued for hours on Instant Message. He always said I was a great friend and a terrible girlfriend. Blah, blah, blah .... If I had trusted him, I would have been a fabulous girlfriend. As it was, he made it very easy to learn things I really didn't want to know, and I was constantly suspicious and searching ... no – not snooping, merely searching for clues into his devious behavior when I wasn't around. (Did he take lessons from Pig Boy?!) Believe me, I found plenty of ammunition to fire him from my life; but for some reason, I couldn't resist him. And even though we both dated other people, we still hung out occasionally.

So I decided to introduce New York to another Chicagoland favorite – Ravinia, which is a summer-long music festival north of the city in a huge, beautiful park. Hundreds of thousands of people flock to their concerts every summer either by car or by train. My friends and I like to pack a picnic with delicious food, wine, candles, and blankets. We find an open spot, spread out our munchies to share, and enjoy music, conversation and a delightful evening. It has become a summer tradition, and I thought I would share it with him. What I thought would be a fun outing turned out to be pure torture for New York – ha! I will now crawl inside his brain and tell the story exactly how I think he would. His perspective always seemed whacked to me, and I was often baffled by it.

Being a new guy in a new city, I met a woman who knew her way around and who enjoyed being pampered in the manner to which I have become accustomed. With a total New York mindset, we did everything at a high level, and I had high expectations for Ravinia. We planned for two days and bought the finest cheeses and wine, prepared salads, olives and other such goods for our picnic. We went out of our way to pick up two of her friends to join us and waited an eternity for them to get into the car with no apologies for their tardiness. Now, me being the anal retentive person I am, I was already offended that they did not value my time considering I was carting these bitches as a favor to the Rocket. (His name for me.)

We drove two hours in traffic as I had to listen to the droning of two mid-30's women discuss their significant others' asses and how reruns of "Sex and the City" were determining the height of current Chicago fashion. No joke, there was a 25-minute discussion on "scrunchies" (whatever the f* they are). One of these women (both teachers) had some sort of bug she caught from her students that made the "bird flu" look like a sore throat. We also went over the musings of the latest Hillbilly music and relationship advice from the Oprah Zombies in my back seat.

Two hours of torture later, we finally arrive at what I think is the venue. Since these jean jacket wearing 4-H rejects made us so late, there was no parking by the actual park, and we had to travel an additional two miles to some elementary school where we were to board a yellow school bus. So I, who ordinarily would valet my car at the front door, had to empty the contents of my trunk (cooler, chairs, blankets, etc.) and sit and wait for a school bus. Not the "FABULOUS" time I had envisioned from all of the things I was told by the Rocket.

So, still being the good boyfriend I thought I was, I didn't say anything as we boarded the bus and even managed to be friendly - even though my tongue was bleeding from all of the biting of it that had to be done on the trip up. We arrived at the entrance to the park and things started to look up. The place was beautiful; everything was green, gorgeous and manicured. Being the city boy that I am, it looked like it was going to be a good time… UNTIL we walked through the gate and I noticed the HUGE "NO SMOKING" signs everywhere. This tickled the Rocket to death, but for me to deal with these Nascar flunkies, the cancer sticks were calling me with a vengeance.

So there I was ... nerves frazzled, nicotine depleted, annoyed, and without enough alcohol to drown these three out. We walked through a veritable sea of people, over hill and dale to find a spot on the lawn miles from ANYWHERE. Then I heard the cojoined squeal of the three girls, "There they are!" where they seem to see someone they know who has space near them. The Rocket was already afraid to look me in the eye knowing I was milliseconds from snapping and ripping everyone a new one.

We set down our spread at this trailer park ho down and settled in. Once unpacked, I quickly realized we could have brought Saltines, Velveeta and Jello squares, and they would have been just as happy. I guzzled my first ten glasses of wine and looked around to NOT see a stage anywhere. Being new to the scene and not wanting to make a fuss for Rocket's sake, I whispered, "Where is the stage?" The reply made me shiver despite the 90-degree heat and 100% humidity I was enjoying.

"Oh, you can't see the stage from here. You need special tickets for that." I could actually see the words in the air as she said them like some comic book. Great.

At this point, I decided to give up and simply survive the rest of the evening as best I could. I excused myself and went the three-mile trek back to the entrance for a smoke. This was the first chance I actually had to look at the people with whom I was sharing this wonderful new experience. To NO surprise, I saw masses of people who looked as though they puttered to this field on their tractors. And I was led to believe this would be a classy, sophisticated, fabulous Chicago experience.

Oh sweet nicotine, please save me! I must have had four cigarettes at once and decided that the wine we had would not be enough, so I went to the concession to look for beer. In approaching the line for the stand, it seemed that I had way too many teeth to get beer, so I walked back to the "group." The Rocket was having a great time and that was enough for me, so I sat still.

Out of nowhere, music filled the air. "Where is that coming from?" was my question to her as she pointed out the speakers located throughout the sod farm where I was sitting. A few bands played that I never heard of, but they weren't the headliner, so the fact that the sounds actually hurt my ears wouldn't deter me from getting through this. THEN COME THE BODINES!!!! OOOH YES, THE BODINES!!!!!! The whole place went nuts, and all I could think of was, "Who the hell are the Bodines?"

Much to my dismay, the masses stood up and started dancing around like some bad hippie version of the summer of love. They knew every word to every song and turned into a zombie-like trance that purely scared me to my core. In the back of my mind, all I could think was, "When can I go to the high crime ghetto area of the city where I feel safer?" I knew for sure in my head and heart that these people were going to break out a special "Kool Aid" and commit group suicide to the hypnotic melodies of the messiahs, THE BODINES. Being adequately buzzed, I actually got up and danced with this wonderful woman in appreciation for exposing me to this life changing experience.

Hours later when the concert ended, it seemed that the polyester pair were adequately drunk and had no interest in packing up or carrying any of the gear that we had brought back to the car. The Rocket would no longer look at me for fear that my stare may turn her to stone, but I was happy to do the packing up just to get the f* out of there and head home. The two others bounced around giddy as schoolgirls and misdirected me back to the parking lot, so while I carried all of the gear, the small trek out (three miles) ended up being closer to five miles. The Rocket was apologizing profusely whenever she could, but it was no help. I was fed up – done – finished – seething.

Trek to bus; bus to car; car to traffic was the next progression furthering this torture that I was starting to think was planned to get even for something I had done to the Rocket in the past. After we piled into the car, the conversation went back to the inane. I was at a point to where an enema and a prostate exam would have been welcome relief, when one of them began to speak about local politics. With my background being in politics, this banter was the last thing I needed to hear. Not only did I weep for the future of our country based on these two teaching our youth, but I had to now be insulted by listening to the political insights of a person who thought that tabloids were the epitome of printed news and current events.

I started to rip into her. The Rocket, trying to keep me from scarring the girl emotionally for life, immediately started to broker a silence between the front and back seats. So for the final 45 minutes of this debacle, all that was heard was the coughing up of lungs from the other one, and I feared for my upholstery.

Anyway, that's the story I believe he would recall. We gals laugh out loud when we revisit the story, and I seriously doubt New York will ever go back to Ravinia. Oh well!

Chapter 26

Indiana and I have started spending more time together. We're both still quite cautious and reserved, but we're having fun! Since he lives in a place that seems like the end of the earth because it's so far away, he always drives to the city to see me and often arrives bearing gifts. He gave me a tape recorder for the times I wake up in the middle of the night wanting to capture a thought so I don't have to scramble for paper, pen and a light; he gave me a hand-painted candleholder in the perfect colors for my condo; he even brought chocolate milk and Oreo cookies ... our favorite snack! He helped me make a fancy two-layer cherry and chocolate cake for a friend's birthday. We go to the movies, to dinner, and for walks. We're slowly warming up to each other, and he is really amazingly patient, kind, caring, and generous.

I sent Stephanie flowers today for Valentine's Day because she's the best sister ever. Besides, every woman deserves a token of love on such a heartwarming and cherished holiday. Ha! My boss and her husband sent me a beautiful floral bouquet and let me go home early so I could get ready for a date with Indiana.

We savored a delicious juicy steak at one of my favorite restaurants, and then he surprised me with center stage, second row tickets to my absolute favorite musical, *Wicked*. I have seen it four times and love it more with each performance ... what a marvelous love story. I get totally involved and cry every time. I went to freshen up afterwards, but it was futile. Poor Indiana had to escort me out into the blazing lights of the lobby that emphasized my red lashless eyes, runny nose, and pale face. Dazzling! What kind of man could possibly love such a troll? Wanting to cheer me up, he made me the proud owner of a pink "Popular" t-shirt with a glittery magic wand. Sure wish I could swirl that wand into a cure for cancer!

Mr. Wonderful

One would think that the Ravinia fiasco would be a cure for my New York addiction, and it nearly was. In fact, it was during one of our numerous non-speaking periods that I met Indiana for the first time. You will recall the story of my friends stopping by to see how he was doing, and I just happened to be with them. The four of us spent an evening drinking and talking in his hot tub. After that introduction, we dated for a little while, but the timing wasn't right.

The summer after that introduction, I produced a play called, "The Benchmark" as a fundraiser for a local organization for whom I volunteered my clerical skills, which somehow evolved into theater production – who knew?! The fictional play follows a homeless man named Mark through three seasons and scuffles at the public library and a shelter, as well as a stint selling StreetWise newspapers. Hours and hours of preparation and effort went into the production with many of my friends stepping up to help, volunteering to participate, and attending. New York and I even had a mutual friend who agreed to play one of the main characters. What a trooper he was!

With only three performances for the event, invitations went out to everyone I knew. Friends brought friends, my family came up to support me, and even Indiana drove over from the edge of the earth to attend, even though we were not dating at the time. He generously treated a group of my gal pals and me to a celebration after the play. While I recognized what a good friend he was, my focus remained on the obviously intentional non-support of a bad friend who still captured my heart. What could I possibly do to win him over? Why did I want to? Even knowing how important this event was to me, New York chose to go out of town for the weekend showing me yet again that I was not a priority in his world. At first I was crushed, then I was livid, and finally I decided he was so self-absorbed and evil that I no longer cared what he did. My goal from that point forward was to ignore him completely. He wasn't worthy of my thoughts, feelings or energy.

As luck would have it, I no longer had to endure seeing or hearing New York at work either. Our company downsized, and he was let go. What a sad day to stand by watching as co-worker after co-worker was allowed a few minutes to pack up their personal items and be escorted out. Not wanting to be next in line, I updated my resume and called my recruiter. Definitely time to move on!

My cousin decided it was time for me to move on and find a good man, so unbeknownst to me, he signed me up for two online dating services. Good grief! Not one to waste an opportunity, I checked it out, spruced up my profile, and started hunting. This could be fun! Unfortunately, one day my fresh profile popped up as an advertisement in New York's email. What were the chances of that happening? Of the gozillions of faces on the internet, how on earth did my profile land in his mailbox? While I did not owe him a moment of explanation, we had quite the heated discussion about it. He was certainly not the boss of me, and I'd show him! I endeavored to become a dating machine until I met my match.

So, of course, I wanted to see who was out there. Mr. Right was surely just a few clicks away! While online sites are a great way to meet people you otherwise would never cross paths with, the process comes with a lot of effort, time, and snafus. As I began meeting some of these potential mates, I quickly learned what I decided was unacceptable behavior:

- If I made plans to meet a guy somewhere and he was late without calling my cell – strike out.

- If he doesn't offer to pick up the tab – strike out.

- If all he does is talk about himself – strike out.

- If all he talks about are all of his bad relationships – strike out.

- If he has poor manners – strike out.

- If he sticks his finger in my food to tell me whether or not it's cooked correctly – strike out!

And if I decide he isn't for me, I casually share that I'm wearing a wig because of the chemotherapy treatments I'm undergoing. You can see the fear wash over their faces, as if they could catch cancer by sitting next to me. I observe in amusement as they scoot away just a tiny bit while their minds start to whirl ... how to escape?! Lost in thought, their eyes glaze over while they guzzle the last of their drink. In a flash, the check is paid, and they're vapor ... sucked under the door and out of my life. Works for me.

What do I want anyway? What is my vision of Mr. Right? All of the relationship experts tell you to be specific when you set your sights on your ideal man: (in no particular order)

* Tall - 6 foot to 6'4"

* *Dark* - *dark hair, tan healthy skin (as opposed to pasty white, rough and scaly)*

* *Handsome – sparkling eyes, great smile, broad shoulders, good posture*

* *Successful businessman – crisp white shirt, well-groomed, ethical, confident leader*

* *Athletic – good physical shape, participates in sports and enjoys going to events*

* *Energetic – no couch potato slouch will be considered*

* *Intelligent – knowledgeable about current events, able to talk about all subjects without being a know-it-all, and be willing to listen to other's points of view*

* *Funny – must laugh often and be able to make me laugh*

* *Thoughtful – good manners, considerate of family, friends, and waiters*

* *Financially Stable – willing and able to pick up tab, enjoys road trips and traveling without whining about the cost, pays bills on time while also being a saver*

* *Geographically desirable – lives within close proximity (walk, bike, cab) or has parking available*

* *Skilled – whether it is playing a sport, driving, fixing things, or giving some love ... a man has to pay attention, be responsible, and take care of business. No ninnies.*

Is that too much to ask?! Stephanie asked me how this list of requirements was working out for me so far. Hmm. That's a good point. I am going to alter my focus to less on what I think I want and more on the person himself. After all, look at me. I'm lucky to be surviving treatments and living my life. How unfair for someone to judge me because I'm not 5'10," my hair is not long and flowing, and I'm too tired to run a 5k. I'm certainly not going to win a beauty contest, but I still bring a lot of yummy treats to the table. Life is full of wonder, and my Mr. Wonderful is waiting to be discovered.

Chapter 27

"If __ever__ you need to talk, vent, laugh, scream, cry on a shoulder, take a break, get away ... whatever! I can and will be there for you."
Handwritten by friend Daniel T.

I did not enjoy treatment #9 today. Everything was routine until the nurse began injecting my first anti-nausea drug. Just like back in the days when I regularly gave blood, I would turn my head and look away so I couldn't see the needle sticking out of my arm. It was just freaky, and I never got used to seeing it. Whenever I was feeling brave and decided to look, I couldn't tear my eyes away. I was mesmerized and unable to respond to the nurse's questions until she covered the insertion point with gauze. Then I snapped out of it and was fine. (And I thought I wanted to be a nurse? Ha!) It's like hearing your voice on the radio when you call in ... you're mesmerized by hearing yourself but you can't listen to the announcer and respond because you're too busy trying to hear what you just said through the delay. It's wacky!

Anyway, during my treatments, they have been sticking the needle into the back of my hand, as opposed to my arm, as the veins are bigger and don't roll away. Even so, sometimes it takes two or three pokes to get the IV to work. The nurse started pushing in the first drug, as she had done eight times before, but it didn't feel right this time. I didn't say anything right away because I thought it must be a fluke feeling that would pass. As I looked down at my hand, the prickling sting I felt was creeping up my arm. I watched in puzzled fascination as red welts began popping up on my hand, wrist, and forearm nearly up to my elbow. Should this be happening? Hardly!

Not wanting to make a fuss, I said, "Um ... I think something's wrong here." I could just imagine my skin burning from the inside out while hard welts formed all the way up my arm, into my neck, and covered my face!!

Stopping the injection immediately, the nurse pulled out the needle and asked, "Are you OK?"

Looking up at her from my perch on the bedside, I responded sheepishly as I didn't want to be a whiner, "Well, not really. My arm is itching like crazy."

She quickly gave me a shot of Benadryl, and the activity ceased. I was so proud of myself for remaining calm, but what a huge relief! However, I then had the joy of rank cottonmouth and grogginess. All the better for my nap. Hee! When I woke up, nothing I could eat or drink would take away the awful taste those drugs left in my mouth. Ick.

Apparently, I developed an allergic reaction to that particular drug. The nurse said only one percent of patients experience this kind of reaction, so it was fun to become a statistic – not! The back of my hand is bruised where the needle went in, but the nurse said that would clear up. If this is the extent of my troubles, I can continue to count my blessings.

Next week is another round of scans to restage the disease. If they find anything, even one problem, I will be surprised. My nurse agreed, as I've been responding so well to treatments. She is so wonderful and really makes me feel like she genuinely cares that I get through this successfully. I am very lucky to have such great care. Still, I can't wait for this to be OVER! I'm so tired.

Give Up Dating

And I became so tired of searching for Mr. Wonderful that I decided to give up. In fact, I decided life was pretty darn spectacular on my own. Nobody eats my food; nobody messes up my bathroom; nobody controls my remote; nobody is the boss of me.

After all, it was not my fault that all the good flowers were already in bouquets and all that was left to pick were the weeds. Believe me, I have been pulling weeds for years and thought they made dandy arrangements. Yet I could never understand why they made my eyes water and my sinuses swell up until I couldn't breathe. I've learned that it takes years of training to acquire the skills to recognize a flower growing in the midst of a field of weeds. If you're lucky, a flower will surprise you and spring up all by itself when you least expect it.

Since I was no longer in the market for weeds, it was time to focus on a new career path and get on with the business of life. My recruiter introduced me to an amazing opportunity in the world of real estate and a new door opened. I jumped in with both feet, took a one-week crash course, and obtained my real estate license. Who knew what a monumental task it would be to support a top real estate producer? I went from a life of leisure to a life of busy, busy, busy!

After six months of learning the business and working like crazy, another summer was coming to a close, and I celebrated my 41st birthday. My lovely boss and her husband treated me to a delightful sushi dinner. Life was good.

It was the very next morning in the shower that I felt a tender spot under my right arm. A swollen lymph gland – typically no big deal – but this time, it was a BIG deal. In fact, it was a big bad monumental deal that changed my perspective on life.

Chapter 28

"We know you have the strength to beat this.
Keep your chin up and lean
on your friends and family.
We love you and are here for you – always!"
Handwritten by friends Pam & Dave

Indiana and I spent the afternoon at the Auto Show. We enjoy looking at all the concept cars and dreaming of what it would be like to drive such a cool car every day. Afterwards, we ate our favorite Chicago pizza and watched the Sunday night television shows. We've been seeing each other for nearly a month, but I only allow him to kiss me on the cheek when he hugs me. I tell him it's only because I have made it this far through my treatments without so much as a cold. And that's true! With a compromised immune system, now is not the time to purposely expose myself to germs. He decided not to be offended by that remark and finds my excuse to keep him at arm's length amusing. To further prevent my catching a cold, he gave me a matching pink hat and scarf – he's so thoughtful! He also gave me a poem written by Phyllis Van Vleck:

My Funny Valentine (A Kiss?)
A kiss can be a quick little peck
On nose, on cheek or even neck
It can also be a meeting of the lips
With action sweet, like gentle sips
But today, it's a "bath" – sloppy and wet
With "who'll swallow who" – cause for a bet
Like hungry piranhas attacking a beef
They gobble and suck beyond belief
They go on and on, as if they can't stop
Sounding like pigs at a trough full of slop

I'll take MY kisses as they "used to be"
Gentle and pleasant – and thrilling me
If kissed like today, I'd yell, "Please quit"
And – "Hand me a towel to mop up the spit."

Wrapped in my new hat and scarf, poem in hand, I allowed him again to kiss my cheek and share a bear hug before he left for a week of golfing in Florida with his buddies. He's a real jewel.

On February 22, 2006, at 7 a.m., I arrived at the hospital for a very important round of restaging tests. Since I was so early, I got a parking space on the second floor and zoomed up to be first in line at check-in. Sporting my new pink hat and scarf, I decided to forego the wig today and just be warm and comfortable in my paper gown. I certainly look like a cancer patient today – no hair, no eyebrows, no eyelashes, pale skin, no make-up, no smile, bundled up to keep warm – what a pitiful sight! I just want to be left alone.

The lobby is huge, and there are about eight other people waiting their turn. I chose to sit in an unoccupied corner so I could privately write in my journal until my name was called. With all the available seats in the room, a lady sits down directly across from me. Cripes – is that necessary? I gave her a scathing glance, crossed my legs, and turned sideways hoping she would move along. Clearly, I don't want to talk to anyone, and I don't want anyone looking at me. She sat there watching me and probably wondering what I was scribbling in my notebook. I can see out of the corner of my eye that she is rubbing her face and staring at me. Good grief. I hope they call my name soon.

This glorious day of testing involves the following orders:

1. Spirometry Flow Volume Coop
2. Bronchodilator Response
3. Lung Volumes
4. Diffusing Capacity
5. Measure Blood 02

Associated Diagnosis: Lymphocyte Rich Classical Hodgkin's Disease

I have had no trouble breathing while exercising or taking the stairs, so I'm certain my lungs are fine. My blood levels have been as expected during chemo treatments. I'm sure everything is fine, but of course it is time to find out. When they called my name, I leapt out of my chair and startled Hawkeye sitting across from me. Ha! Made me chuckle – she must think I'm deranged. That's ok – I think she's a little odd herself.

The technician was the same gal who tested me before. Without my saying a word, she closed the door this time – thank you very much. She ushered me into the booth and promptly clipped a clamp on my nose, which immediately took my breath away. For the next 15 minutes, I took deep breaths, exhaled quickly for as long as I could, and went through a series of breathing exercises over and over and over.

At the end, I asked, "Am I normal?" As if.

She said, "Everything looks fine." Whew! What a relief.

I blew my nose three different times during the process, as my nose tends to drip these days with no hair to stop it, and I blow my nose all day long. Gross. I never realized nose hair actually serves a purpose.

The tech asked, "Are you back at work?"

"I have never missed work, except for appointments."

She raised her eyebrows and batted her eyes in disbelief. I think a lot of other patients just get tired, and maybe sick, and stay home from work, so I said, "I'm just lucky I guess."

She concluded, "Since you have an office job and don't do a lot of running around, you must not need as much energy to work." Ha! She has no clue, but believe me, I set her straight.

They ushered me back into the lobby where I had to wait until the next round of tests – Gated Heart, Planar, Single. Apparently, I need this because I am receiving anthracyclines in my chemo treatments. Again, I am so thankful I am at the best cancer center in the city.

As I sat quietly waiting with a half dozen other people, a staff member walked right up to me when they were ready for me. How did she know it was me? They did the same thing for everyone here instead of calling out our names. We're not wearing nametags, so how did she know? Guess that's one of life's little mysteries that can continue to baffle me. Actually, I enjoy not figuring out and analyzing everything – just like I never try to figure out who dunnit at the movie or try to guess how it ends. I prefer to enjoy the show as it unfolds.

After I changed into another gown, again I sat quietly in another lobby waiting for my turn and had time to ponder. My hand still hurts from the injection reaction. The pain reliever I took last night helped, but the problem does not appear to be healing. I ate Girl Scout cookies for breakfast before I swallowed the day's pile of pills. Probably should have eaten oatmeal instead since I won't have time to eat all day. I don't understand why my fingernails and toenails are growing so fast all of a sudden. I've become a clipping and filing fool!

At 9 a.m. a nurse called me into her office to sign some forms and answer questions.

"No, I'm not pregnant."

"Yes, I've had this test before."

She took me to another room where a different nurse expertly inserted an IV, gave me a dye injection, and had me wait 20 more minutes in a freezing room while the dye circulated through my system. Back in my high school days, our church did a fundraiser at a meat packing plant that smelled a million times worse than the pig barn at the fair – a stink so strong it could knock you down. We had to stand inside that freezing stinky room for hours and stuff frozen hot dogs into a bun, then into a foil wrapper, and into a cardboard box to be sold at concession stands at the college football games. Before that, I never gave one moment's thought to how a hot dog arrived at the stadium. Needless to say, hot dogs no longer pass by my lips unless I'm absolutely starving and there is nothing else to eat.

Waiting in that freezing hospital room, I looked around and was thankful not to see or smell anything peculiar. They are going to take pictures of my heart, so I get to lie down during that scan and take a nap. Will I dream about hot dogs?! Good thing I have my scarf & hat to keep me warm. Thanks, Indiana. Wonder how well he's golfing this week.

Another nurse took me into a room so cold I could almost see my breath. Hot dogs had to be in there somewhere! Actually, there was a big eCAM around a narrow, hard table that I had to climb onto like a balance beam. How do large people manage? I felt slightly goofy in my hat and scarf, but I was not about to take them off. In fact, I wished I had mittens and my poncho! The nurse brought two deliciously warm blankets, one to lie on and one to cover me. Once tucked in, the nurse asked me to pull my arm out from under the blanket so she could draw blood, let it mix with their solution, then inject it back into me. She then placed a couple stickers with wires attached on my chest, slid the table down to the camera, and started taking pictures. Each session took about eight minutes.

I closed my eyes and tried to relax, but couldn't fall asleep. Visions of hot dogs danced through my head ... not. I was too busy thinking about how to make more money so I could afford to buy a condo with a lake view. There must be a way!

Chapter 29

"Just wanted to let you know that my prayers are with you. You are a strong woman, all will be OK!! If I can help you in any way, please let me know."

Handwritten by co-worker Dan A.

Apparently, I fell asleep. The nurse woke me up and led me to a different waiting room. Next is a 12:30 p.m. PET scan and last will be a 3 p.m. CT scan. All this shuffling around is exhausting. At least I can see out the window to enjoy this bright, sunny 40-degree day. Every day is better when the sun is shining!

Through the window, I can see a construction crew outside tearing down a building across the street. A lot of men are walking around very close to a big yellow machine that is hacking away at the structure. Out with the old before you can bring in the new. Reminds me of a song I learned in Brownies as a 2nd grader. "Make new friends, but keep the old, one is silver and the other is gold." We sang that song over and over and over. Funny how I can remember that from 35 years ago, but can't remember how many square feet are in a mile, and I just learned that a year ago when I was studying to get my real estate license.

From my childhood, I still remember the 4-H Pledge, too:

> "I pledge my head to clearer thinking;
> My heart to greater loyalty;
> My hands to larger service; and
> My health to better living for
> My club, my community, my country, and my world."

I had to show cattle and pigs during my 4-H career. Hence, the reason I know exactly how stinky a pig barn is. My dad was the Leader, and I don't remember this club being an option. And as if washing, grooming, and trying to get a stubborn animal to walk around the showroom in a circle weren't torture enough, we had to give speeches to our fellow 4-Hers. My best speech, and the only one I even remember, was on the value and use of the telephone book. Even today, the phonebook remains a valuable resource.

12:20 p.m. Here we go, checking in for a PET scan for restaging. Yipes! I pray, please let's not find anything. Please. I am getting hungry now that I know I can't eat or drink anything. What a horrible feeling it must be to really starve – I have no idea, as I am so spoiled. If I feel hungry, I get food and eat. I am so thankful. Right now, I would really like a chopped salad and an ice cold cola. Guess I'll have to wait for dinner.

12:45 p.m. A smiling, perky male nurse retrieved me from the waiting room. He led me into a private room with a reclining chair. First, he tested my blood sugar level – 100% perfect. Who said you can't eat cookies for breakfast?! He left the room and brought back a dosage of radiation based on my height, weight, and whether I am left or right handed. That's weird, but OK. The injection material was inside a very nuclear protective looking canister, and I'm sure they must be required to limit their exposure to that poison. Using the IV from my last injection, he quickly gave me the shot, gave me a couple of blankets, took out the IV, and told me to relax for about 40 minutes while this circulates through my system. Then we'll go for more pictures. Nap time!

A horrible daytime talk show was on the TV. Before he left the room, I asked him to shut it off, which he did, and then bounced out of the room with a smile on his face. He must truly love his job and his life. Perhaps he got a little love last night. Good for him – we should all be so cheerful.

Times up. Cheerful came back to take me down the hall to yet another room and strapped me to a long, narrow table for the PET scan. Jazz music played in the background, blankets kept me warm, and I dozed off again. An hour later, the tech determined that the pictures were good, so they escorted me down the hall to wait for the CT scans of my chest, abdomen, and pelvis.

I was still hungry. As luck would have it, the hospital provided drinks! I got to enjoy two delicious Berry Smoothie Readi-CAT2 barium "milkshakes." They gave me 30 minutes to drink the first one and 30 minutes for the other one timed so that I finished 10 minutes before they called me. I couldn't quite get all of the second one swallowed before they swooped me into the hall and down to the scanning room. I laid down on another long hard narrow table, but no blankets this time, as the scan only took five minutes. Pictures looked good – I was excused. Can't wait to hear positive results.

Since these treatments are just about over, and I'll be getting on with the business of living my life to the fullest, it's time to set some new goals. What do I want?

1. Circle of diamonds pendant
2. Electric blanket
3. 2 bedroom/2 bath condo with a view of Lake Michigan
4. Lose 10 pounds
5. The LOVE of my life

Now, these aren't crazy goals. I do have control over some things, others not so much. But, they are now out there in the Universe, and I believe they are attainable.

Indiana is coming over tonight before he leaves for Las Vegas. He sure has set himself up with a fun life. I know he lived without many things in the past and has worked really hard to get where he is today, so he deserves to have a fun, good life! I'll share my goals with him and see what some of his goals are. He's such a good listener and sounding board and is becoming a really excellent friend. Who would have thought?

Chapter 30

*"I hope this is the last card asking you to 'get well soon' that you ever receive!
I am thrilled to hear the news and can't wait 'til all side effects are gone!"*
Handwritten from my friend Katie

Big Day! During treatment #10, I weighed in at a few pounds less than last time – woohoo! I can totally lose 10 pounds if I just get some more exercise, eat more yogurt and fewer cookies. Even better news is that I am in remission, as expected! Only three more treatments and I'll be done!!! To celebrate, I treated myself to a manicure and pedicure on the way home – love that. The bruise on my left hand is still dark and red, so no more injections in that hand. The manicurist didn't ask me what it was, but she gave it a good look, and I'm pretty sure she was impressed with my pencil eyebrows.

Stephanie used to make fun of me for always trying to shape my eyebrows into an arch. I'd pluck out the extra hairs and was constantly pushing my index finger into the spot on my brows where I wanted the arch – they can be trained after all. Now I simply draw them on, and I have a perfect arch!

Plus, a few years ago I spent an entire year of torture and hundreds of dollars being zapped with a flash of light to remove the hair from my knees, shins, and bikini area. Don't ever let anybody tell you it doesn't hurt! Now I have no hair and haven't had to shave in five months.

My nails are perfect and my skin glows like never before. What's going to happen when chemo is over, my body chemistry goes back to normal, and I'm not taking super pills every day? Sure is going to be interesting.

Indiana is coming back from Vegas this weekend, and I am going to kiss him hello. He will be so surprised! I think about him a lot, and he doesn't call too much. He's doing everything right. In fact, with his encouragement, I am going to start the process of getting pre-qualified for a new mortgage and start shopping for my dream condo. If I'm going to stay in Chicago, I want to see the lake every day from my dining room table. Fun!

As has become our routine, Indiana came over Sunday night, and we did exchange a little kiss and a lot of conversation. He's very candid, and we talk about everything. He makes me laugh with some of his questions, mostly about past relationships. Why on earth does he want to know these things? I certainly don't. He told me he loves me, and I just looked at him in wonderment. How is that possible? Does he love me or is he just in love with the idea of being in love? He's very open and honest, caring, faithful, hard working, energetic, athletic, intelligent, successful ... everything I declared I wanted in Mr. Wonderful. I'm afraid to be too excited about him, as we haven't been together all that long and time tells true character. I remain reserved until I feel in my heart that I can trust him completely.

Treatment #11 passed uneventfully. Indiana asked if he could come to my next treatment – I'll only have two left after that. He wants to see where I go, what they do, and how it works so he can understand better what I'm going through. Sure, it would be nice to have his company, especially when most people avoid going to the hospital at all costs. He also asked if I want to go to Colorado for a few days the weekend after next. The company he sells for has their corporate office in Golden. He needs to have a meeting with them, and then we can spend a few days in the mountains shopping, dining, and treating ourselves to a spa. I haven't been anywhere in ages -- sounds like fun!

Meanwhile, we have been condo shopping. We walked through new construction that we both thought was ideal, and we could pick the finishes. By the time the Realtor called me back, it was under contract. And yes, I say we, as I value his opinion, and I'm guessing he'll be spending quite a bit of time with me wherever I choose to live. I'll be putting my condo on the market shortly and see what I can get for it after having lived there for five years – time flies I tell ya.

Time for treatment #12. Indiana met me at my office for lunch with my co-workers, as has been their gracious custom since the beginning. He drove me to the hospital and absorbed the process. Once the treatment was underway, he reached into his coat pocket and pulled out a little maroon box tied with a gold ribbon. With a sly smile, he handed me this gift. What could it be?! I was stunned, as his taking the time and even wanting to be there with me was gift enough. Inside the box was a gorgeous two-circle of diamonds pendant. One of the items on my Wish List! To make it even more dazzling, he had written a poem that I read through misty eyes:

> *The ring or circle, throughout time, has been a symbol of completeness and unity. It is often associated with womanhood and mother earth. It is no coincidence that the symbol of marriage between husband and wife is outwardly demonstrated by the wearing of rings. Some consider the circle to be the perfect form, no beginning and no end, complete within itself.*
>
> *Kelly, in just TWO more treatments, you will have come "full circle," from health to illness and back to health again. You will be "complete" again, proving what a strong woman you are.*
>
> *To a lesser degree, we have also come "full circle." Once together, then apart, and now we are together again. After having met TWO years ago, I am very happy to have a second chance to share my life with you.*
>
> *So, today I give you this gift. Not a symbolic circle alone, but TWO to represent your journey to completeness in more ways than one.*
>
> *Thanks for letting me share your day!*

How could I not love and trust someone who would do this for me? I'd be a fool to let him get away from me again. He is a wonderful man. I am so lucky.

Chapter 31

"You did it!! ... You have endured chemotherapy with strength, grace and style. You're amazing."

Card from my friend Malissa

I'm exhausted and sitting in the Denver airport nursing a sore throat covered with white spots. Swallowing razor blades is not my idea of a good time. My nose drips like a leaky faucet. I'm miserable and cold, then hot, then cold. I'm a train wreck and quite pleasant to be around, to be sure.

Indiana generously treated me to a lovely weekend in Breckenridge. We stayed at a beautiful spa resort in the foothills. As promised, we shopped, dined and enjoyed strolling in the crisp air and bright sunshine. After our very first afternoon, we were so worn out that the moment we sat down to rest, our eyelids drooped, our heads bobbed, and we could not stay awake. In fact, we napped right through dinner. The next day, we had an early appointment for a massage and a steam. Then we walked and shopped some more. He bought me a gorgeous turquoise necklace and got himself a pair of Oakley sunglasses. By mid-afternoon, I had developed a sore throat, and he was suffering from altitude sickness. What a delightful pair!

Back in Chicago – I can't get out of bed to go to work. I can't eat because I can't swallow. I'm exhausted but don't sleep well because I can't breathe. When I do fall asleep, I wake up with cardboard tongue from my mouth gaping open. Gross. I guess flying the friendly skies was premature, and I should have waited longer before exposing myself to all those travel germs. Indiana feels terrible that I'm sick, but it's not his fault. I should have known better. Oh well.

After a couple days of sleeping upright, coughing and blowing my nose, I'm feeling much better. Indiana took me out for dinner to meet his oldest son. Just like his brother, he is absolutely darling, sweet and polite. Indiana is a great father and friend to his boys – their relationship is open and loving. I'm so happy for them, yet selfishly sad for me that I'll never get to experience being a mom. I waited too long. Alas, my pursuit of Mr. Perfect was to my detriment. Can't change that, so might as well get on with my life as best I can.

So, I signed on the dotted line and bought my dream condo! It has everything ... two bedrooms + den, two full bathrooms, balcony, unobstructed lake view, in-unit washer/dryer, stainless appliances, granite counters, indoor parking, workout room, rooftop deck and pool. Since it is new construction, it won't be ready until the fall, which means I have six months to sell my current condo. Next week, I'll put it on the market and cross my fingers.

April 12, 2006 .. a magical day! I enjoyed my last group luncheon at work and a celebration party in my hospital room with Stephanie, our friend Marianne, and Indiana for my final treatment. We consumed cupcakes and champagne – two of my favorites. Indiana brought three pounds of Rocky Mountain chocolates that should melt in my mouth for the next several months ... yum!

Everything went smoothly, and I couldn't wait to leave the hospital. My boss called when I got home to say congratulations. I am emotionally exhausted and so relieved. I have my health back and am surrounded by wonderful people who care about me. My future is bright and will be full of great new adventures.

Two days later, I'm still exhausted. I can't wait to fall into bed after work. When will I get my energy back? When will my hair start to grow back? When will my hand heal? Why do my toes go numb when I walk? Why do my toenails have black spots? Why does my left arm ache now? Apparently, my body doesn't know that I am DONE with chemo. Done, I say! Guess it takes awhile to recover, and it's no cakewalk.

Stephanie and I invited Indiana home for Easter to meet my brother and The Kettles. Of course, they all love Indiana – what's not to love? He's a solid man with Midwestern values and youthful good looks. He's kind, intelligent, conversational, interesting, and a good storyteller who makes everyone laugh. The consensus is ... he's a keeper! To hear Indiana tell it, we are a good match because he chose me. I just had to learn to appreciate him, accept my good luck, and trust that he is genuine.

And as luck would have it, I put my condo on the market and accepted an offer on the 10th day. Wow ... gotta love that! I am one lucky person, except now I'm homeless until the new condo is ready. What to do, what to do? Such a dilemma.

With all the evil in my life having been replaced by goodness, I have again been blessed. My first Chicago roommate and her husband have opened their home to me until my new condo is ready. Not only will I have my own room and my own bathroom, I will have the pleasure of babysitting their 3-year old triplets once a week so my friends can enjoy a date night. While most definitely a handful, they are adorable, energetic, happy children. What a fun summer it will be!

Chapter 32

*"You're a "SuperStar!"… that's what you are! Congratulations!
So glad you made it and this is over. Here's to a fabulous
FUTURE!!"*

Card from Stephanie

Summer 2006 began with a trip to Puerto Vallarta to celebrate with Stephanie and some of our gal pals. Off went the wig for a few days of sun and rejuvenation! I still look like a bald cancer patient, but the road to recovery is paved with joy regardless of my appearance. The rest of summer was filled with trips to the beach to jet ski, cookouts, movies in the park, outdoor concerts, ballgames, and golf.

One of Indiana's greatest passions is golf. Because he has supported and cared for me when times were bleak, I wanted to support him in his endeavor to be the best golfer he could be. One day on the course, he ruined a brand new expensive golf shirt. He wasn't really bothered by the incident, but unbeknownst to Indiana, I decided to take action on his behalf and wrote the following letter to the company in New York.

Dear Bobby Jones Collection:

Enclosed is a gorgeous golf shirt from your collection made of the finest 100% cotton material I've ever touched. My boyfriend is an avid golfer and is having the best summer of his career. As a special gift to wish him good luck and continued success (and hopefully a club championship!), I splurged on this fabulous shirt … dress for success! He was so surprised and absolutely loved it — recognizing the brand name and superior quality — he could not wait to wear it in last weekend's golf tournament.

Bright and early, he sped off to the golf course dressed like a pro in his fabulous Bobby Jones golf shirt with a feeling of pride and confidence. He would rule this round. His partner was duly impressed, as he recognized the excellent brand of the new shirt, and with good karma, they set out to be winners! My boyfriend teed off excited about playing his best while looking so hot, yet staying so cool.

Near the end of the front nine, he made a highly unusual shot into the trees. He went in search of his ball and spying it, bent down to pick it up. As he stood up, a thorn latched onto the front of his new Bobby Jones shirt and snagged the fabric. What?! Much to his complete dismay, he could see a thread sticking out. The nerve! You can't have a snag on the front of your excellent, brand new, first time out, Bobby Jones shirt ... so he grabbed the thread and yanked. Yipes! The thread pulled out and ripped open the front of his shirt worse than a run in my stockings. He was mortified! One nasty little thorn had created a huge, gaping hole that exposed his belly, ruined his wonderful gift, and put a damper on his spirit for the rest of the day. His new Bobby Jones shirt was destroyed! Inconceivable.

In the sweltering heat for the rest of the day, he wore a jacket over his once magnificent Bobby Jones shirt. He could not comprehend that a tiny snag and the unfortunate tug of a string would tear his shirt apart. He felt horrible having to tell me that this expensive, thoughtful gift, one he was planning to enjoy for years, was damaged beyond repair, never to be worn again. When he told me what happened, I couldn't help but think that a company who makes such high quality, superior clothing would stand behind their product.

While I recognize that his shirt is ruined because of an unfortunate twist of events, not a manufacturing defect by your fine company, I am reaching out to you in the hope you will consider our plight. I could have purchased three ordinary golf shirts for the price of one spectacular Bobby Jones Collection shirt, but I wanted my boyfriend to have the BEST and wear it with pride because he is the BEST man I've ever had the privilege to know.

We would both be deeply touched and forever loyal in the promotion of the Bobby Jones Collection if you would consider replacing his extravagant garment. I'm not asking for a refund or a credit, I'm simply asking that you grant him the privilege of wearing one of your amazing golf shirts.

With all due respect and admiration –

I mailed his ruined shirt with my plea and hoped for the best. I had nothing to lose and a new shirt to gain! Nearly two months later, I received a package in the mail from the Bobby Jones company with the enclosed reply:

Dear Miss:

I am in receipt of the Collection Knit Shirt that you had returned to our offices. Your well-written account of what happened caught my attention and prompted me to address the situation.

As noted, this is not a manufacturer's defect; however, I will be more than pleased to replace the garment for your boyfriend. As I must return the garment you sent to us, a replacement garment from our current collection will be sent under separate cover from our distribution center.

Thank you for taking the time to forward the enclosed garment and for your loyalty to the Bobby Jones brand.

> *Best regards,*
> *Vice President of Customer Service*

Well, howdy doo … we not only got his old green shirt back, but we actually received a brand new blue one! And to further show Indiana how much I cared, I spent several hours one night hand stitching his ruined shirt back together. Only the very discerning eye can tell that anything is askew. He was so taken aback by my efforts, this man of a million words was speechless. He is now the proud owner of two very fine golf shirts from the Bobby Jones Collection and realizes there isn't anything I wouldn't do for him. He is the love of my life.

Chapter 33

"You have been so strong that honestly I'm not surprised you beat it! Your spirits, your will, your attitude, your efforts were always visibly more than 100%. You give the rest of us something to strive for!"
Note written by co-worker Lisa G.

One year has passed since my first treatment, and I seem to be doing very well. My hair is growing back curly! Never in a gazillion years would I have thought my hair would be anything but stick straight. Quite frankly, it's growing back evenly and in such a way that it looks like I actually cut it this way. Who knew?! My eyebrows are back and no more arched than they ever were – rats! All those years of training wasted. My eyelashes are back just as long and plentiful as before. I have gotten so out of the habit of shaving, I forget all about it when I'm in the shower. No big deal – I'll do it tomorrow.

Time for another PET scan and CT scan to make sure my insides are managing as well. We'll do this every four months for two years, then I will be in the clear. If I were to have a reoccurrence, they tell me it would have happened already most likely. STILL ... we've got to take some pictures to confirm that I remain cancer free.

My left hand is scarred for life, I guess. Every time I study the back of my hand, I remember where I've been and how far I've come. Life is good now, and I'm so lucky to be happy, healthy, in love and loved in return.

Indiana, Stephanie, our friend Molly, and The Kettles helped me move into the new condo ... LOVE it! The place is a dream come true. I skip around barely containing myself at times. Once I accidentally kicked a closet door off its hinges as I leaped down the hallway! Yet, here I sit at my dining room table, watching the cars whiz by on Lake

Shore Drive, enjoying the sailboats as they drift on Lake Michigan, and hearing the roar of a Bears game. Without the help of my boss and the support of a good man, this would not have been possible.

My love and I established a weekly routine of being together on the weekends, whether in Chicago, Indiana or out of town, and each Wednesday is date night in Chicago. We either make dinner together and watch TV, go to a movie, go out for dinner – sometimes with friends, or attend a ballgame, theater or an event. We're not picky about what we do, as long as we do it together. This leaves Monday, Tuesday and Thursday nights available to do as we please. For two people who have lived independently for years, our schedule works like a charm! Understand that this arrangement only works because I have finally met a man that I trust 100%, and I never have to worry for a single moment about what he might be up to when I'm not around. He's the best, and my life with him is happy, peaceful, and a dream come true.

Since I am one of the first to move into the building, the elevators are functional but not pretty, the lobby and hallways aren't finished, and we're not allowed on the rooftop deck. One blustery winter night when I got home from work, Indiana was waiting for me and suggested we go up to the rooftop to check on progress before we go out for dinner. Mmm, ok. Much to my surprise, when we approached the door to the outside deck, it was propped open. What's going on here? I gave Indiana my best puzzled look without saying any words. He seemed edgy and was sweating bullets even though it was January and freezing outside. Is he sick? What's wrong? He doesn't seem well. Does he have something to tell me? Oh boy.

I wasn't prepared to go outside and didn't have a coat. But we stepped out onto the deck into the biting wind and looked at the breathtaking view of the city – WOW. This is going to be a wonderful place to spend time together when it is ready. Shivering from the cold and ready to go back inside, I looked at Indiana as he was fumbling through a speech he must have prepared … I didn't hear a word he said because I was distracted by the little maroon box tied with a gold ribbon that he pulled out of his pocket. My heart stopped beating as he said the words, "Will you share the rest of your life with me?" My heart overflowed with the warmth of love as we hugged and kissed, and of course I said yes.

We planned to exchange vows four months later on that same spot on the rooftop deck with 75 of our closest friends and family. However, three weeks before the wedding, we were informed that the deck/pool would not be completed, so we would not be allowed to use it. Yipes ... now what?! Indiana had obtained special permission for our engagement, but they could not make an exception for a wedding ceremony and reception. Having already mailed our invitations, we had to switch gears, find another location, and mail out a change of venue card. Brother! We had to scramble to find the best alternative.

Little did Indiana know that he was about to make another one of my dreams come true. For years, I thought if I ever got married again, I wanted to be like The Little Mermaid and marry my prince on a yacht at sunset. As luck would have it, The Mystic Blue at Navy Pier was available on the Saturday of Memorial Day weekend. Our costs just doubled, but hey – how often do I get to be a princess bride? I am so lucky!

We booked the yacht, as they graciously allowed us to continue with the fabulous caterer we already paid, our harpists, our soloist (my brother!) our flowers and decorations, and our moist and delicious wedding mini-cupcakes. Indiana spent hours and hours downloading the perfect songs on his iPod for our reception, and they had just installed a new docking station. With detailed spreadsheets to coordinate activity, each member of my family was assigned a task for set up and take down to assure a smooth and perfect event. We were even blessed with an afternoon of light rain to keep the temperature cool. Could it be any more delightful?!

Just minutes before our wedding ceremony began, my wonderful girlfriend Pam, who introduced me to Indiana four years ago, gave me a brightly colored box to open. Inside was The Little Mermaid in a wedding dress with a card from her five-year-old daughter that said,

> *"My mommy told me that you feel like Ariel today!*
> *(I love Ariel!) You are getting married to your handsome*
> *prince on a boat at sunset! I wish I could see you! You are*
> *our Princess Ariel Bride!*
> *Love, Sissy (and Mommy too!)"*

She was exactly right, and I was deeply touched by her thoughtful gift, as it broke her little heart to give away her prized Ariel. Overwhelmed with emotion, tears rolled down my cheeks as I hugged my friend, and they didn't stop for about three hours.

My beloved and I wrote our vows, and as I suspected would happen, I couldn't see through my tears to read. As I held Indiana's hands and looked into his eyes, Stephanie stepped up and spoke for me:

> *Today I officially join my life to yours, not merely*
> *as your wife, but as your best friend and companion for*
> *the rest of your life. You've been told your life is over, but*
> *actually, the best part of your life has just begun.*
>
> *I am amazed that we found our way to standing here*
> *today, and I think it's wonderful. Because you're wonderful.*
> *As you have stood by me through some hard times, so will*
> *I be a light in your life to support you through laughter*
> *and through tears. You know I cry tears of joy and you*
> *understand me. I love you for that.*
>
> *And I love that you are patient, kind, generous and a*
> *great dad. I've never known two boys more openly loving*
> *than yours, and that's because of you. I am so blessed to*
> *become a part of your family.*
>
> *As you have encouraged me to follow my dreams, from*
> *buying a new condo to starting a new career, so will I promise*
> *to share and support your hopes, your dreams and your goals.*
> *Together we will build a great life, always remembering to*
> *lift each other up no matter how hard it gets.*
>
> *As you have chosen me and love me, so do I choose you*
> *and love you. I promise to stand by you always, but above*

all else, I promise to allow you to be you – the golfer, the ATVer, the jet skier, and whatever you decide to do next.

Everything I am and everything I have is yours, from this moment to eternity.

Then it was his turn to declare his promise to me:

Wow ... throughout history, smarter men than me have likened life to a journey. I stand here in amazement that our journeys have brought us to this moment. I'm humbled as I look around me, seeing great friends, loving family, and you, my bride, and the opportunity that is before us. I know it is cliché to say ... well actually I think it is becoming cliché to say it's cliché ... but anyway ... you complete me. We compliment each other ... go together so well, not like oil and water ... more like water and water ... or oil and oil ... you are the water to my water. I guess I'm saying we blend well.

Back in January, I asked you to share the rest of your life with me. But it's more than that. I not only want to share my life, but do everything in my power to make your life absolutely wonderful. Today I give you my heart.

We were pronounced husband and wife -- Daniel and Kelly Molchan. We shared our first kiss, the music started, food and drinks were served, cupcakes and champagne were enjoyed, and the season's first fireworks lit up the sky. What a glorious beginning!

During the reception, Dan's boys gave a toast and Stephanie shared a poem she wrote for us:

For Dan and Kelly
A Poem by Stephanie Entitled
"I Am Usually Right!"

It all began a couple of years ago, when they were introduced by friends,
But the timing wasn't right and against MY advice it all came quickly to an end.
I, personally, really liked Dan, so much more than all the rest,
But unfortunately for all of us, he had not passed the "Kelly" test.
With his endless observations, quick wit and boyish charm,
I thought he could be the last one she took home to the farm.
Their second encounter came during a very dark time,
The dreaded "C" word had entered our lives and things were not fine.
The romance began again with a simple "Thinking of You" card,
Followed by a lunch and things suddenly didn't seem so hard.
It was like they both were seeing each other in a whole different light,
The planets seemed to align and things were going to be alright.
Kelly with her strength, endurance and bizzbuzz ways,
Along with Dan's calming support, there could only be brighter days.
So Dan, when you lose your Monday, Tuesday, Thursday, don't be too sad,
You are gaining so much more and you both will be so glad.
I know you love her, and I certainly hope you can afford her,
And even though I am the younger sister, once again, I knew I was right!

Good does triumph over evil and confirms my motto:

Live ... Laugh ... Love ... Enjoy!

About the Author

Kelly Molchan has been a professional legal secretary and executive assistant for over 20 years. During that time, she married, divorced and then began dating again. Amazingly unbelievable stories evolved from the men she met! For years friends have encouraged her to write about these crazy adventures. While under the knife during a lymph node biopsy, she decided now was the time to review years of journals and calendars, reflect on each of her erroneous relationships, and write this memoir.

Nearly everyone today is touched by cancer. You may have a friend, relative, co-worker or even a friend of a friend who has been diagnosed with some type of cancer, but you never believe it will happen to you. This is the story of a strong, otherwise healthy, active woman's journey with cancer and her analysis of its cause: the toxic accumulation of 20 years of dating the wrong men!

"Having undergone discovery of the tumors, diagnosis of the disease, and application of the treatments, I still marvel at the mystery of getting cancer, living with it, and being cured of it while so many others suffer and are not blessed with the gift of remission. I am sharing these very personal memories as I remember them, along with information on Hodgkin's Lymphoma, in the hope of helping readers understand what a person with cancer endures. After all, surely the negative effects of my quest for love caused my cancer. How else could this disease have grown inside me?! I hope my words reach out and touch your heart, encourage and give strength to those who are struggling with cancer in any way, and provide a chuckle or two reminding everyone that laughter is the best medicine."

Kelly currently lives in Valparaiso, Indiana, with her husband, Dan.

LaVergne, TN USA
18 August 2009

155094LV00004B/5/P